Enter Papa Nosedrop waving a huge ugly object. From the sky all sorts of valuable objects begin falling and sailing. Shirts, shoes, coats, girdles, bras, electric thises and thatses. The contents of the whole Sunday Edition!

STORE DAYS

Documents from The Store (1961)
and Ray Gun Theater (1962)
Selected by Claes Oldenburg
and Emmett Williams
Photographs by Robert R. McElroy

1967
SOMETHING ELSE PRESS, INC.
New York / Villefranche-sur-mer / Frankfurt am Main

To Poopy

L. C. Catalog Card No: 67–16292

Manufactured in the United States of America

7   I want these pieces to have an unbridled intense satanic vulgarity un-surpassable, and yet be art. To work in total art is hard as hell.

      yellow banana truck

Manifesto of an Artist N.Y.C. 1961

Good morning
My wife's back
Latin songs
Dropped bags of crap
Dropped iceboxes
Smashing glass
My wife's hair
Cat's meows
Firecracker blasts
Pigeons coo
Cars starting up
My wife's tough tits

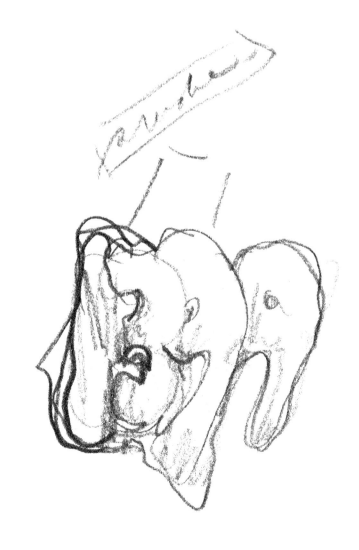

thick enamel pt.

Dolores' pants

A new definition of NY is needed you see and that is why New York will be renamed Ray-Gun

this country is all bourgeois down to the last deathtail and most of the **8**
criticism is an exhortation to observe art and justice and good sense and
humanity, which are also bourgeois values, so there is no escaping bourgeois
values in America. The enemy is bourgeois culture nevertheless.

CITY AX or TAXI
Torrent
tame
torrential
hat song
hot seng
bed

If I could only forget the notion of art entirely. I really don't think
you can win. Duchamp is ultimately labeled art too. The bourgeois scheme
is that they wish to be disturbed from time to time, they like that, but
then they envelop you, and that little bit is over, and they are ready for
the next. There even exists within the b. values a code of possibilities for
disturbance, certain "crimes" which it requires some courage to do but
which will eventually be rewarded within the b. scheme. B. values are
human weakness, a civilization built on human weakness, non-resistance.
They are disgusting. There are many difficult things to do within the b.
values, but I would like to find some way to take a totally outside position.
Bohemia is bourgeois. The beat is bourgeois——their values are pure sentimentality——the country, the good heart, the fallen man, the honest man,
the gold-hearted whore etc. They would never think f.ex. of making the
city a value of good.

Possibly art is doomed to be bourgeois. Two possible escapes from
the bourgeois are 1. aristocracy and 2. intellect, where art never thrives
too well. There again I am talking as if I want to create art outside b.
values. Perhaps this can't be done, but why should I even want to create
"art"——that's the notion I've got to get rid of. Assuming that I wanted
to create some thing what would that thing be? Just a thing, an object.
Art would not enter into it. I make a charged object ("living"). An "artistic"
appearance or content is derived from the object's reference, not from the
object itself or me. These things are displayed in galleries, but that is not
the place for them. A store would be better (Store——place full of objects).
Museum in b. concept equals store in mine.

9   Problem is probably with gas on stomach which causes symptoms described, lying flat on cold surfaces f.ex.   Dr. suggests giving Charlie mineral oil (not Cod Liver Oil), either by dropper & spoon in mouth, or by mixing with food. He said castrated cats are apt to develop "crystals" in their bladder if the diet is too strictly fish (Puss and Boots etc.), and recommended giving him liver, kidneys, any kind of meat (therefore not Cod Liver Oil). He said if condition does not improve, bring cat back for enema. In next few weeks watch his bowel movements, note if constipated. He appeared constipated at the hospital, Dr. felt his bowels. As for skin thing, he gave a test for one kind of fungus but it wasn't that. Gave me (sold me) some·ointment to put on lesions, pluck out loose hair or cut it away and rub this stuff in, do not lay on too much or Charlie will lick it off. Very nice place & Charlie well behaved. Cost cabs .80 apiece——1.60 and visit 3.25. Total 4.85. . . .

thankyou

i always smile while riding a horse

Egypt

Well that is it: the sun goes up and one starts to work. Then is one either lucky or not lucky. And one isnt lucky every day & some days get a bad reputation, like Thursdays.

Here in the ruins, we take matter for the spirit from what sources we can. Our study of asphalt having exhausted the joys therefrom, we move to the excellent representations provided for us in full color, which are brought down and put on our walls and especially in the stores, and the beautiful goods which fill these stores.

The US peacetime as a crisis situation.
A kind of expressionist expressive commercial art.
But dont take the ruins away. Theyre the only good thing.
US always represented in crisis situation by me. New York best for this.

Study Bras

I dont consider myself in struggle w nature but in harmony w her. Neither arrogance nor humility but harmony and identification. Nothing is not nature (natural?) and nothing not suitable for the living organizational capacity which is "art". That which everyman does when walking down street artist does as an act in itself and therefore as a model to others.
Taking on as many problems as he can.
"Beauty" is word of praise for his successful effort.
The multitude of natural possibilities prevents its having any single definition.
An artist is a specialist in synthesis of physical practical world.
He analyzes or breaks up only to rearrange and ultimately to resynthesize.

Fig/non fig is moronic distinction. The challenge to abstract art must go much deeper.

The plaster in my bathroom is very nice
same goes for the hall, which is now being
painted with shiny enamel
Theres a lot of noise from the house
in back but we like it even if the guys all sing
off key at once. New York wouldnt be much
without Puerto Rico
Now and then the ferris wheel on the truck comes
down the street or the ice-cream truck with its
ship-bell
My wife comes in and twists my nose and
That is how it goes

thats better   my style has been going to hell

13   I have got love all mixed up with art. I have got my sentiments for the world all mixed up with art. I am a disaster as an artist because I cant leave the world alone.

The limitation of space forces me to consider making only smaller pieces at home.

Larger pieces, which i want to make, not solved as to where. Build Monuments in places f.ex. take over places, like a store and build from there or more conventionally share some place or rent it?

    Lately I have begun to understand action painting that old thing in a new vital and peculiar sense—as corny as the scratches on a NY wall and by parodying its corn I have (miracle) come back to its authenticity! I feel as if Pollock is sitting on my shoulder, or rather crouching in my pants!

dog barks
cat meows
rain

twinkles
cymbals
distant band

    I will not be dragged off to the country again. To please pat, who then doesnt like it anyway. Cows and shit. It may just be that i get interrupted which fucks up the summer and fall.

What is a big object well that is a room. I have no desire to do environments but I will do a room, I am turned on by the thick plaster and green paint of a kitchen in my neighborhood. The accumulation and mystery. The heaped up table with a radio in it. Something frying on the stove. The other stuff ought well be saved for later.

plaques (flags)
monuments
space forms (whitmans)
houses——rooms

objects in tombs (Egypt)

I want my form and color to arise out of my experience, not be artistic like Jimmys.

anExpOSe of AllAn KapRow

The store windows I see now serve as models for clusters——eye-clusters——formal model for a kind of visual experience: fragmentation, simultaneousness, superimposition, which I wish to recreate in the clusters.

perhaps free clusters in air & not only of plaster. enamel plaster?

Women must work
men must think and eat
will i be held on labor laws?

A show——! forget the commercialism and vanity of the long-prepared show. A show is the gesture of being alive, a period——before as well as during. . . . a look into one's continuing daily activity.

actually make a store!
14 st or 6 ave
butchershop etc
the whole store an apotheosis!

a sad, past, hi(stor)ical store
a happy contemporary store too?

The store will have a counter
All the objects will be three-dimensional
There will be fragments of walls
chairs etc.

for billy, some shit money

The Store, or My Store, or the Ray-Gun Mfg. Co., located at 107 E. 2nd St., N.Y.C., is eighty feet long and varies about 10 ft wide. In the front half, it is my intention to create the environment of a store, by painting and placing (hanging, projecting, lying) objects after the spirit and in the form of popular objects of merchandise, such as may be seen in stores and store-windows of the city, especially in the area where the store is (Clinton St., f.ex., Delancey St., 14th St.).

This store will be constantly supplied with new objects which I will create out of plaster and other materials in the rear half of the place. The objects will be for sale in the store.

The store will be open every day at hours I will post. F.ex. AM 10–2, PM 5–7, or the hours when I will be able to be in the store, which is also of course my studio.

The store may be thought of as a season-long exhibit, with changing & new material. It will be the center of my activities during the season.

The rent of the store is $60.00 per month, including steam heat and hot and cold water. Additional money will be needed to paint and plaster the front half and to make objects. Rent for 10 mos.——$600. Additional money to equip store——$150. Money to make objects——$250. ($24 per month). Total $1000.

RAY GUN MFG CO

DECIEMBRE 1 AL 31

THE STORE

By

Claes Oldenburg

107 E. 2ND ST.

MANHATTAN PRESS 1602 PARK AVE. LE 4-7977

RAY-GUN MFG. CO.

DICIEMBRE 1 AL 31

THE STORE
BY
CLAES OLDENBURG

107 E. 2ND ST.

HOURS: FRI., SAT., SUN. 1 TO 6 P.M.
AND BY APPOINTMENT
IN COOPERATION WITH
THE GREEN GALLERY

MANHATTAN PRESS 1662 PARK AVE. LE 4-7977

13 Incidents at the Store

A customer enters
Something is bought
Something is returned
It costs too much
A bargain!
Someone is hired. (someone is fired.)
The founders. How they struggled.
Inventory
Fire sale
Store closed on acct of death in family
The Night Before Christmas
Modeling clothes
A lecture to the Salesmen

1. A Customer Enters

The room is dark. A man sits at the table. Two female bodies on the floor. A hand hangs down from the "attic". The light is very dim. In the slowest possible gesture, the man lifts the telephone to his ear. The bodies move a little.

The hand returns to the attic. Sound of the MickeyMouse banjo.

2. Something Purchased

The lights come on again, dimly. The man is still at the table talking into the phone (not saying anything). Another man enters very briskly, takes off a heavy winter coat and hangs it on a hook, then freezes. Both the man with the phone and the other man are frozen.

The hand descends to drop a glassful of water.

3. A bargain!

Sound of the man upstairs reading a paper (ie. turning the pages). Everyone as they were. A red paint begins to run down around the walls from the attic. Coughing upstairs.

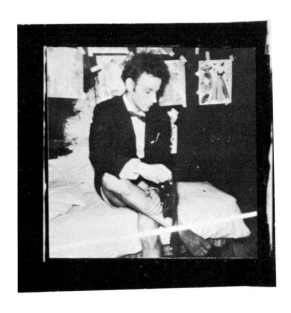

4. How the Founders Struggled.

All as it was.

The man (woman) from above lowers himself slowly to his waist and hangs there. The telephone rings time after time. The neighbor begins practising trumpet. Bass drum and tambourine.

A man enters with a surprised look on his face. He takes off his glasses and freezes.

The (man) upstairs pulls himself up again.

5. Store closed on account of death in family.

Laughter is heard from upstairs. A number of small objects fall out of cracks and holes from above. A little snow. The man with the phone as slowly as before puts it down, and the man with the coat sinks to the floor in imitation of the gesture.

Snoring from above.

The bodies on the floor wriggle.

One of the women on the floor is pulled slowly up by a rope into the attic so that her underwear shows, upside down. The rope continues to the other girl.

The man at the phone falls slowly forward.

The man with the glasses is slowly covered with a bag.

Saxophone plays.

6. A lecture to the Salesmen

The head of the (man) in the attic comes down upside down smoking a cigarette. He is lowered to the floor where he collects in a heap. The girl stands up, very alert, brushes her skirt, puts on gloves.

Rapid counting from upstairs.

Sound of a cashregister. Trumpet plays.

The girl pushes the man by the table so that he falls. She sits down and writes a long note.

The covered man with glasses leans more and more forward until he is at a fortyfive degree angle and remains frozen there.

The girl kisses the pieces of paper she is writing and stuffs them into her dress after writing on each piece and kissing it. She freezes.

A red light, then a yellow light.

(A nose blown.)

A blue light. Long motionlessness.

end

The goods in the stores: clothing, objects of every sort, and the boxes and wrappers, signs and billboards——for all these radiant commercial articles in my immediate surroundings I have developed a great affection, which has made me want to imitate them. And so I have made these things: a wrist-watch, a piece of pie, hats, caps, pants, skirts, flags, 7up, shoe-shine etc. etc., all violent and simple in form and color, just as they are. In showing them together, I have wanted to imitate my act of perceiving them, which is why they are shown as fragments (of the field of seeing), in different scale to one another, in a form surrounding me (and the spectator), and in accumulation rather than in some imposed design. And the effect is: I have made my own **Store.**

Atget corset shops
That flat shirt form the found object too see how it gathers to a form relief and bulging planes   pillows
an adjective for the sawmill?
little gestures: ear tweaks
                    to talk into hair held up

the matter of reaching certainty   not yet
how to get these new forms and colors into my systems of feeling
so that f.ex. brilliant simple color is sad
and not (which is what it usually is) happy
i always set myself problems

the ads are nearly an absolute equivalent of the stores themselves
window or store equals ad
      gas main   powerhouse   garage
color technique subject has all come together after two mos prep
lumberyard   papermill   printing   plant
rags of c.   age of fabric   clothes rags
Eventually I hope the metamorphic and creative takes over from the realistic as the present takes over from the past.
the gothic mythopoeic vision
      closline white sale

My life is a history of rooms in which I am self-locked in. My life is also a history of frantic "escapes" which come to nothing, back to a room. So, accepted.

This limits my expression to "my reality", that is, to an "artists" reality. I know my separation.

I have had something like affairs with rooms. Goodbyes f.ex. Union only with impersonal nature.

This room, enclosure is my natural attraction to environments which I conceive as interiors or even if open: high ceilings or enclosed outside (the street)

My work is thoroughly and honestly self-projective, narcissistic. This "weakness" constitutes its power. My desire for an audience is the desire to confess, a desire to reach, or be reached, be saved from enclosure. Which never happens.

Noone reaches me. I reach noone, except thru disguises and thru others (players)

My form of writing is either autobiographical——descriptive of my procedures f.ex. or subjects; or fantasy. Objectivity is really beyond me and my detachment is not that, but separation. Opinions are my weakest area, so I put these in letters that is personal statements and freely which like statements spoken may thus be discredited by being momentary and subjective and contexted

Store——Eros

The Store is like the Street an environmental (as well as a thematic) form. In a way they are the same thing because some streets or squares (like TSq) are just large open stores (windows, signs etc.). In The Store the concentration upon objects is more intense, and harsh colors rather than greys and browns dominate.

Guises of RG   ie. like Christian faith forced under ~~xxxxxxxxxxxxxxxxxxxx~~ ^{any} ~~xxxxxxxx~~ system to dwell in disguises

As the artist in his disguises

As art in its disguises

As the power of seeing truth   in its disguises

As the self   in its disguises

As religion   in its disguises

Ray-Gun is both a form of deception (to everyone, incl. oneself) and a form of play. so important play is.   ie. only the comic is serious. only the off-hand is effective etc.
Therefore, Ray-Gun is a series of contradictions, paradoxes. A form of dialectic.

Ray-Gun as Eros or life   in its disguises.

Its disguises are very often its opposites.
Ray Gun is ultimately the unknowable, pursued futiley through all its dis guises, yet the sine qua non.
The amnibguity the slipperiness of its definition is not a problem but it essence...from a mortal view.
It is a faith, or the possibility of faith, which is whyhitsreligious r p pings and refs to mystical ~~and christian~~ theory.
It is the essence or need for religion beyond existing ~~xxxxx~~ machinery

Rg as the street. Rg as the store. Rg as the factory !

fireplace is altar

some perfs are mystical "seances"

burned my fjinger and wenttost vinvcent

cla3s w lef6 hand

Inventory of Store Dec. 1961

1.	9.99 free hanging	$399.95
2.	39 cents relief	198.99
3.	**Store Ray-Gun** free hanging	249.95
4.	**Success Plant** free standing	249.99
5.	**"To My Love"** Inscription from Cake relief	149.95
6.	**Cash Register** free standing	349.99
7.	**U.S. Flag Fragment** relief	297.95
8.	**Bunting** relief	149.99
9.	**Times Square Figure** free standing	149.98
10.	**Statue of Liberty Souvenir** free standing	169.98
11.	**Funeral Heart** relief	349.98
12.	**Store Cross** relief	399.98
13.	**Wedding Bouquet** free hanging	229.89
14.	**Bride Mannikin** free standing	899.95
15.	**Injun Souvenir** free standing	124.99
16.	**Toy Ray Gun** free lying	34.99
17.	**Mannikin with One Leg** free standing	499.98
18.	**Auto Tire with Fragment of Price** relief	449.69
19.	**Iron Fragment** relief	449.95
20.	**Sewing Machine** relief	449.99
21.	**Rings Fragment** relief	199.98
22.	**Wrist Watch on Blue** relief	295.98
23.	**Cigarette and Smoke** free hanging	99.95
24.	**Girl, Flag, Cigarettes** reliefs on wood	198.99
25.	**Cigarettes in Pack Fragment** relief	499.99
26.	**Pepsi-Cola Sign** relief	399.98
27.	**Oranges** relief	279.89
28.	**Orange Juice** relief	199.95
29.	**Plate of Meat** relief	399.98
30.	**Bacon & Egg** relief	229.95
31.	**Big Sandwich** relief	149.98
32.	**Red Pie** relief	399.95
33.	**Small Yellow Pie** relief	169.99
34.	**Four Flat Pies in a Row** free standing	149.95

35.	**Ice Cream Bar** free standing	169.99
36.	**Ice Cream Cake** relief	169.99
37.	**Ice Cream Cone and Heel** relief	124.95
38.	**Red Sausages** relief	199.98
39.	**Chocolates in Box** (*Fragment*) relief	399.98
40.	**Stockinged Thighs Framed by Skirt** (*Stocking Advertisement Fragment*) relief	299.95
41.	**Four Flat Panties in a Row** free standing	149.95
42.	**Blue and Pink Panties** relief	349.99
43.	**Green Stockings** relief	169.95
44.	**Blue Legs** relief	299.99
45.	**Green Legs with Shoes** relief	299.99
46.	**Black Girdle** relief	249.95
47.	**Red Tights with Fragment 9** relief	395.99
48.	**Braselette** relief	299.95
49.	**Fur Jacket with White Gloves** relief	324.95
50.	**Small Beauty Parlor Face** relief	49.99
51.	**Large Beauty Parlor Face** plasterboard on wood plaque	69.98
52.	**Pink Cap** relief	299.89
53.	**Two Hats** relief	249.99
54.	**Dress Jacket** enamel on plaster on paper	49.95
55.	**Man's Shoe** relief	199.99
56.	**Mu-Mu** relief	449.19
57.	**Blouse** projecting relief	299.95
58.	**Three Ladies' Stockings** free hanging	99.99
59.	**Black Ladies' Shoe** free mounted	125.95
60.	**Yellow Girls' Dress** relief	249.99
61.	**Red Cap** free standing	199.95
62.	**Man's Sock** free hanging	199.95
63.	**White Gym Shoes** free standing	129.99
64.	**Ties** free standing	129.99
65.	**Blue Shirt, Striped Tie** free standing	149.95
66.	**Men's Jacket with Shirt and Tie** free hanging	399.95
67.	**Jacket and Shirt Fragment** relief	249.99
68.	**Big White Shirt with Blue Tie** free standing	399.95
69.	**Big Necklace** free hanging	199.95
70.	**Ear-rings** (*drop form*) free hanging	44.98

71. **Watch in a Red Box**   free standing   129.95
72. **Two Girls' Dresses**   relief   349.99
73. **Counter and Plates with Potato & Ham**   free standing   279.98
74. **Cakes in a Glass Box**   free standing   324.98
75. **Candy Counter with Candy**   free standing   399.97
76. **Candy Bar**   free lying   49.95
77. **Four Pies in a Glass Case**   249.99
78. **Blonde Pie**   free standing   149.95
79. **"Vulgar" Pie**   free standing   124.95
80. **Flat Long Pastry**   free standing   169.99
81. **Strawberry Shortcake**   free standing   84.95
82. **Big Chocolate Cake**   free standing   149.98
83. **Half Cheese Cake**   free standing   149.98
84. **Cheese Cake**   free standing   124.99
85. **Striped Cake Slice**   free standing   44.95
86. **Cherry Pastry**   free standing   44.98
87. **Shell Cookie**   free lying   (w. plate)   29.95
88. **Cube Pastry**   free standing   24.98
89. **Three Jelly Doughnuts**   free lying   99.99
90. **Plate of Assorted Pastries**   free standing   124.99
91. **Two Danish & Turnover**   free lying   (w. plate)   149.95
92. **Two Loaves of Bread, One Cut**   free standing   349.99
93. **Sandwich**   free lying   74.98
94. **Pile of Toast**   free lying   149.89
95. **Carrots**   free hanging   99.98
96. **Liver Sausage & Slices**   free lying   149.95
97. **Fried Chicken (2)**   free lying   99.98
98. **Sardine Can with 2 Sardines on Paper Bag**   free standing   124.97
99. **Roast**   free lying or hanging   179.98
100. **Fried Egg in Pan**   free standing   34.98
101. **Roses on a Plate**   free lying   49.95
102. **Match Cover**   free lying   44.98
103. **Cigarette Pack**   free lying   49.95
104. **Air Mail Letter**   free lying   74.99
105. **Post Card**   free lying   39.95
106. **Calendar**   free hanging   79.89
107. **Oval Photograph**   free   21.79

chair
rings
dresses
candy
skates
buggy
kool-aid (glass)
eyeglasses
stocking
vacuum
curtains

slippers

lettering

tires

umbrellas

cigars

teeth

crossword puzzle

bulb

garterbelt ?

shoeshine

SUN SHU

I am for an art that is political-erotical-mystical, that does something other than sit on its ass in a museum.

I am for an art that grows up not knowing it is art at all, an art given the chance of having a starting point of zero.

I am for an art that embroils itself with the everyday crap & still comes out on top.

I am for an art that imitates the human, that is comic, if necessary, or violent, or whatever is necessary.

I am for an art that takes its form from the lines of life itself, that twists and extends and accumulates and spits and drips, and is heavy and coarse and blunt and sweet and stupid as life itself.

I am for an artist who vanishes, turning up in a white cap painting signs or hallways.

I am for art that comes out of a chimney like black hair and scatters in the sky.

I am for art that spills out of an old man's purse when he is bounced off a passing fender.

I am for the art out of a doggy's mouth, falling five stories from the roof.

I am for the art that a kid licks, after peeling away the wrapper.

I am for an art that joggles like everyones knees, when the bus traverses an excavation.

I am for art that is smoked, like a cigarette, smells, like a pair of shoes.

I am for art that flaps like a flag, or helps blow noses, like a handkerchief.

I am for art that is put on and taken off, like pants, which develops holes, like socks, which is eaten, like a piece of pie, or abandoned with great contempt, like a piece of shit.

I am for art covered with bandages. I am for art that limps and rolls and runs and jumps. I am for art that comes in a can or washes up on the shore.

I am for art that coils and grunts like a wrestler. I am for art that sheds hair.

I am for art you can sit on. I am for art you can pick your nose with or stub your toes on.

I am for art from a pocket, from deep channels of the ear, from the

edge of a knife, from the corners of the mouth, stuck in the eye or worn
on the wrist.

I am for art under the skirts, and the art of pinching cockroaches.

I am for the art of conversation between the sidewalk and a blind mans metal stick.

I am for the art that grows in a pot, that comes down out of the skies at night, like lightning, that hides in the clouds and growls. I am for art that is flipped on and off with a switch.

I am for art that unfolds like a map, that you can squeeze, like your sweetys arm, or kiss, like a pet dog. Which expands and squeaks, like an accordion, which you can spill your dinner on, like an old tablecloth.

I am for an art that you can hammer with, stitch with, sew with, paste with, file with.

I am for an art that tells you the time of day, or where such and such a street is.

I am for an art that helps old ladies across the street.

I am for the art of the washing machine. I am for the art of a government check. I am for the art of last wars raincoat.

I am for the art that comes up in fogs from sewer-holes in winter. I am for the art that splits when you step on a frozen puddle. I am for the worms art inside the apple. I am for the art of sweat that develops between crossed legs.

I am for the art of neck-hair and caked tea-cups, for the art between the tines of restaurant forks, for the odor of boiling dishwater.

I am for the art of sailing on Sunday, and the art of red and white gasoline pumps.

I am for the art of bright blue factory columns and blinking biscuit signs.

I am for the art of cheap plaster and enamel. I am for the art of worn marble and smashed slate. I am for the art of rolling cobblestones and sliding sand. I am for the art of slag and black coal. I am for the art of dead birds.

I am for the art of scratchings in the asphalt, daubing at the walls. I am for the art of bending and kicking metal and breaking glass, and pulling at things to make them fall down.

I am for the art of punching and skinned knees and sat-on bananas. I am for the art of kids' smells. I am for the art of mama-babble.

I am for the art of bar-babble, tooth-picking, beerdrinking, egg-salting, in-sulting. I am for the art of falling off a barstool.

I am for the art of underwear and the art of taxicabs. I am for the art of ice-cream cones dropped on concrete. I am for the majestic art of dog-turds, rising like cathedrals.

I am for the blinking arts, lighting up the night. I am for art falling, splashing, wiggling, jumping, going on and off.

I am for the art of fat truck-tires and black eyes.

I am for Kool-art, 7-UP art, Pepsi-art, Sunshine art, 39 cents art, 15 cents art, Vatronol art, Dro-bomb art, Vam art, Menthol art, L&M art, Ex-lax art, Venida art, Heaven Hill art, Pamryl art, San-o-med art, Rx art, 9.99 art, Now art, New art, How art, Fire sale art, Last Chance art, Only art, Diamond art, Tomorrow art, Franks art, Ducks art, Meat-o-rama art.

I am for the art of bread wet by rain. I am for the rats' dance between floors. I am for the art of flies walking on a slick pear in the electric light. I am for the art of soggy onions and firm green shoots. I am for the art of clicking among the nuts when the roaches come and go. I am for the brown sad art of rotting apples.

I am for the art of meowls and clatter of cats and for the art of their dumb electric eyes.

I am for the white art of refrigerators and their muscular openings and closings.

I am for the art of rust and mold. I am for the art of hearts, funeral hearts or sweetheart hearts, full of nougat. I am for the art of worn meat-hooks and singing barrels of red, white, blue and yellow meat.

I am for the art of things lost or thrown away, coming home from school. I am for the art of cock-and-ball trees and flying cows and the noise of rectangles and squares. I am for the art of crayons and weak grey pencil-lead, and grainy wash and sticky oil paint, and the art of windshield wipers and the art of the finger on a cold window, on dusty steel or in the bubbles on the sides of a bathtub.

I am for the art of teddy-bears and guns and decapitated rabbits, ex-ploded umbrellas, raped beds, chairs with their brown bones broken, burning trees, firecracker ends, chicken bones, pigeon bones and boxes with men sleeping in them.

I am for the art of slightly rotten funeral flowers, hung bloody rabbits and wrinkly yellow chickens, bass drums & tambourines, and plastic phonographs.

I am for the art of abandoned boxes, tied like pharaohs. I am for an art of watertanks and speeding clouds and flapping shades.

I am for U.S. Government Inspected Art, Grade A art, Regular Price art, Yellow Ripe art, Extra Fancy art, Ready-to-eat art, Best-for-less art, Ready-to-cook art, Fully cleaned art, Spend Less art, Eat Better art, Ham art, pork art, chicken art, tomato art, banana art, apple art, turkey art, cake art, cookie art.

add

Im for an art that is combed down, that is hung from each ear, that is laid on the lips and under the eyes, that is shaved from the legs, that is brushed on the teeth, that is fixed on the thighs, that is slipped on the foot.

square which becomes blobby

Photo: Art Freed

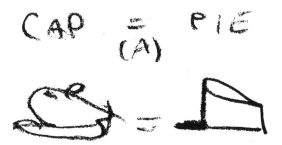

CAP = PIE
(A)

Vocabulary

Glass: 1. Eye. 2. Separations: Inside/outside. Examples: Store window. Pastry-cases.

Ray Gun: 1. kid's toy. 2. Seeing through walls. 3. The universal angle. Examples: Legs, Sevens, Pistols, Arms, Phalli——simple Ray Guns. Double Ray Guns: Cross, Airplanes. Absurd Ray Guns: Ice Cream Sodas. Complex Ray Guns: Chairs, Beds. 4. Anagrams and homophonies: Nug Yar (New York). ReuBen (Gallery). 5. Accidental references: A moviehouse in Harlem. A nuclear testing site in the Sahara (Ragon). 6. What ever is needed. A word ought to be useful. 7. Cryptic sayings: "All will see as Ray Gun sees." "The name of New York will be changed to Ray Gun." "When Ray Gun shoots, noone dies." 8. Talismanic, fetishistic functions.

Store: 1. EROS 2. Stomach. 3. Memory. Enter My Store.

Volume

Increased flatulence.
Model: a balloon. Pressure from center out. From inside. Skin over matter straining out.

Technique of increased flatulence: stuffed cloth. Reversed seam.

Correspondence and likely subjects: toys (FAO Schwartz)

Line turned in. Dissolution turned in. No outline, no agitation. Continuous, complacent, tight skin like a man swollen with water.

Repeat (as with line and color): I always make things bigger or smaller than they ought to be. (but sometimes just the same size)

Color

A chunk in space. 1. leaving its surface 2. free.
(drawing: irregularity of nearness against simplicity of distance)
painting: melting pitted against sustaining. Droops.
(drawing: edge vs. area)
painting: dissolution vs. volume. Ice. Butter. Vegetables. Ice Cream.
Cloth in the wind.

Techniques: plaster, body paint (enamel).

Correspondences: pastries, textiles, all kinds.

Likely subjects (therefore): food, clothing (as in windows)

Line

Coastlines, drawings of an imaginary country. Edges, plains or cliffs where
the land meets the sea (matter/space, flesh/space). The empty part of
the paper is torn off and thrown away. The drawn part (the land) is hung in
space.

Cardboard found on the street 1. is cheap 2. makes nice coastlines.

The source of line is the street.

Plane

Rising (if flat) or swelling from an edge, like the wing of an airplane.
Stuffed or held out (as by wire covered with paper). Floating. Plane should
be able to be seen from side and in the many pts of observation from side to
front, as with Moon. The plane is a distortion of a sphere or cube through
vision.

Shadows, silhouettes, illusions, perspective.

I use naive imitation. This is not because I have no imagination or because I wish to say something about the everyday world. I imitate 1. objects and 2. created objects, f.ex. signs. Objects made without the intention of making "art" and which naively contain a functional contemporary magic. I try to carry these even further through my own naivete, which is not artificial. Further, i.e. charge them more intensely, elaborate their reference. I do not try to make "art" out of them. This must be understood. I imitate these because I want people to get accustomed to recognizing the power of objects, a didactic aim. If I alter, which I do usually, I do not alter for "art" and I do not alter to express *myself*, I alter to unfold the object, and to add to it other object-qualities, forces. The object remains an object, only expanded and less specific.

There is first the ice-cream cone as it is. This would be one imitation. Then begins a series of parallel representations which are not the ice-cream cone but nevertheless realistic or objective: f. ex. the ice-cream cone in a newspaper ad. The ice-cream cone or any other popular shape as a fetish object. The ice-cream cone in altered scale (giant). The ice-cream cone as a symbol etc. Only the created object——my parallel cone——will include and/or concentrate several of these.

The fact that the store represents American popular art is only an accident, an accident of my surroundings, my landscape, of the objects which in my daily coming and going my consciousness attaches itself to. An art of ideas is a bore and a sentimentality, whether witty or serious or what. I may have things to say about US and many other matters, but in my art I am concerned with perception of reality and composition. Which is the only way that art can really be useful——by setting an example of how to use the senses.

49   I know that down to the last simple detail experience is totally mysterious. The only person I know that tried to prove the simplest thing in the world, like a piece of candy, was utterly mysterious was Chirico (in his early days). But I guess its what every still-life ptr worth anything tried to show too. With me of c. well I am living in the city, a particular city, in a different time, and my subjects are as apt to be depictions of the real thing as the real things (even real pie these days does not taste like pie). Still, what I want to do more than anything is to create things just as mysterious as nature.

The form here is not so much environmental as fragmental. The fragments are different as to scale and time, though they are all related. You are to imagine the missing, that is, what is called negative space or absent matter, counts for something. These are rips out of reality, perceptions like snapshots, embodiments of glances.

(There isn't a thing you can say about art that doesnt sound like corn!)

Goods are exalted. The joy that people find in goods, which takes them out of their ciphrous existence as consumers. Goods as a metaphysical mystical "Supply". Simple bright goods are exalted, proletarian goods.

a touch of line and dot makes such a difference

The Store
may be better understood if it is considered not itself a psychological statement but a collection of psychological statements which exist concretely in the form of signs and advertisements. Placement and relation unfixed, free. An imitation not of nature or nature in the city but nature altered toward psychology, which is to say: the true "landscape" of the city.

It is important to me that a work of art be constantly elusive, mean many different things to many different people. My work is always on its way between one point and another. What I care most about is its living possibilities.

The original idea of The Store was a simple one——to fill a space with objects such as those in any kind of store, but this was not satisfactory as I proceeded. The problem became how to individualize the simple objects, how to surprise them——fragmentation, gigantism, obsession. My piece is called a store because like a store it is a collection of objects randomly placed in space.

one's own body the form of change
keep form even after making, in a situation of change
not only mechanical but psychological
moving sculptures are often all fixed
mine are not
the law of my work is time
                    change

cock and balls
cock and balls equals tie and collar
equals leg and bra   equals stars and stripes
flag equals cigarette package and
cigarettes

heart equals balls and triangle
equals (upside down) girdle and stockings
equals (sidewise) cigarette package equals
flag

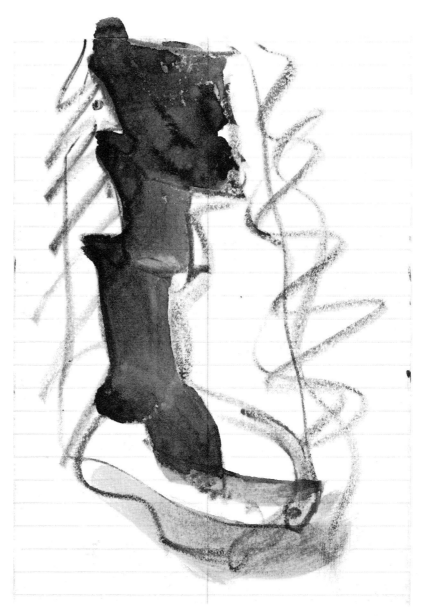

  The store tries to overcome the sense of guilt connected with money and sales which the artist has——either inherited or to rationalize his lack of ability to make money. It is to say money is life (like Bossman) it is plenty . . . it is psychological . . . articles are child or substitute . . .
  Commerce is organic and psychological
  Thus again, unity——no separation between commerce and art

Transvestitism of garment industry
sewing is an art isn't it

53   Evanescence is not just a theory it is part of me. Come and go. Nothing I do is a theory but is me.

a girl with long dowellegs and white stockings, a cherryred dress, mailing a letter

a kid with sleeves of white shirt rolled up tapping ashes from his cigarette on the stone steps

shirt fragment
black fragments
white duck
cars
planes (subs)
piece of clay (day)–
landscape =

beach
blot (plot)

monuments to love
tombs to love
buried behind glass
the store windows
the store cases

windmills
invisible forces
piglet
goose
boat
puppet show
house white
    full of lite

The store expresses a kind of contempt or disinterest in color, or it expresses the expansion of color into form in space, that is the super texture supercollage. My theme is here as often the expansion of ptg into actual space, towards sculpture, and the puns about illusion, which is actual and actuality which is illusion. The relation of painting and sculpture from the vantage pt of sculpture, whereas jim's vantage point is painting and he expresses contempt for sculpture. That is his jokes are about building without architecture.

food = love
metrecal = death of love

i have just had an insight
red is redder than green, meaner than yellow, and
bloodier than black

The flag in color equals the free painting (both cloth)

My idea of an environmental piece is that quite a large area (the larger the better) ought to be controlled——and any thing and all who enter this space——by certain radiating pieces or clusters of form and color. This conception for me involves both the power of pure form and color and also my belief in magic. A great deal of trial and error and thought and care goes into making certain that these centers do their work.

my art is a resolution of opposites:

strives for a simultaneous presentation of $\begin{cases} \text{contraries} \\ \text{opposites} \end{cases}$
in subj the ordinary and the extraordinary
in form the aesthetic and the unaesthetic
solidity and bodylessness
pathos and indifference
mystery and commonplace
etc.

Cloth, dipped in plaster
Dropped on chickenwire
Painted with enamel

This is paint vs. sculpture.

spitball singterror

down manhole roll firehose

mousetail grey photothief

The heaped up table with a radio in it. Yxx Something frying on

the stove

coakand balls equals tie and collar equals leg and bra equals stars

and stripes

flag equals cigarette package

heart equals balls and triangle equals (upside down) girdle and

stockings equals (sidewise) cigarette package equals flag

Ironworks - arms race

Who is the bum the rag man in my dreams

Store windows as models for clusters Eyeclusters

 New York - paper and plaster Chicago - metallic SF - vaporous

P-town - woody

Keep the store open a half year and then sell it whole. Have it

transferred to bronze

Just now I am indulging my femininity

I want these pieces to have an unbridled intense satanic vulgarity

unsurpassable, and yet be "art"

Yellow bananatruck

Art must be savage and magical

Menaces and presences of death. memorials and charms to keep

death at bay. In surveying experience which I aim at I find I

must assign death a large role. I like Celines constant sens of

death

I want the plaster to be like the 100 year accumulation in every

slum bathroom or kitchen

Potatoes our specialty. Night: persons dressed as junk lie in

the lot

smaller pieces determined by scraps

everything ought to be used f. ex. if one has a wife

at last a gallery a useful lively place

imitation of garment shops

rainbows
taxicabs
patent leather
dust
monuments (in the sun)

i wanted to see if i could make significant form out of a pair of ladys pantys.
toothbrush   small leg

My approach is a direct strong vulgarity
Lisztian Beethovian Bruegelian Orozcoan Whitmanian Rabelaisian
including delicacy

    This elevation of sensibility above bourgeois values, which is also a simplicity of return to truth and first principles, will (hopefully) destroy the notion of art and give the object back its power. Then the magic inherent in the universe will be restored and people will live in sympathetic religious exchange with the materials and objects surrounding them. They will not feel so different from these objects, and the animate/inanimate schism mended. What is now called an art object is a debased understanding of a magic object. When our vision is clouded by bourgeois values and by removal from an actual functional situation (through museum-civilization) the power of the object wch was a functioning object becomes suspended and only its artificiality, that is its craft and design (which are the lowest and easiest of creations), are noted. This is "art." Think how many children a day are being perverted into art and their natural recognition of the magic in objects stamped out!

fragments

The erotic or the sexual is the root of "art", its first impulse. Today sexuality is more directed, or here where I am in Am. at this time, toward substitutes f.ex. clothing rather than the person, fetichistic stuff, and this gives the object an intensity and this is what I try to project.

As everyone might know . . .
No, everyone doesn't . . .
I operate, idea-wise, far above the ground, but I have a compulsion (which is not the desire for respectability) to relate myself to what is on the ground, regardless of the distortion or attack on my ideas which this inevitably results in.
That is in fact——the store
Ethically I see no reason to remove myself from life, how can one? and still be ethical . . .
It is a necessarily losing battle, undertaken *of my own free will* (which is important). I think it is necessarily a failure.

pleases me to be uselessly (for its own sake) methodical and systematic (especially as an artist who is in the cliche not so) like the world of business science engineering sales
will i sentimentalize 57th St. too
In place of chance——
whimsical or useless activity
satire is not the word

Why do I not just present the real thing instead of imitating it? Because my desire to imitate extends to the event or activity of making the thing I imitate. In one instance that is to be for a moment a sign-painter, in another, for a moment a baker of cakes, in another the cutter of suits, etc. etc. In some cases especially, but really in all, it is necessary to be for a moment nature herself, if this is possible. In handling plaster and enamel I was behaving like the painter who was at the same time painting my stairway. When I carry my plaster and paints up the stairs, the neighbors assume I am improving my home.

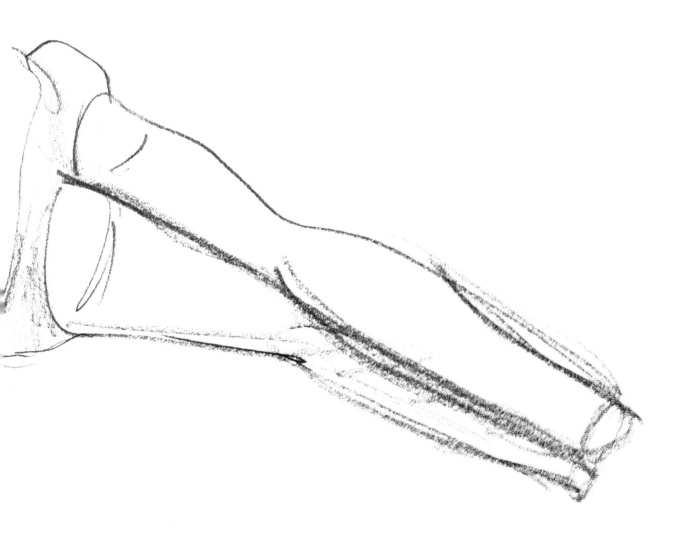

In The Store I am naively reconstructing an act of vision, a kind of literal-scientific approach. (Here again the analogy of the lightning trapped in sand applies).

I am impure. I am feeling and skill. It might even be said of me that I corrupt by my presence.

I have not remained unintellectual but uninformed. Apart from ideas.

absurd imitations (i.e. useless) of perfectly sensible and useful pursuits.

absurd carpentry   dressmaking etc.

1 0 7 ٤ 2 ٦٢

It is important to operate out of the forces in us, forces and counter-forces and not to be afraid to use them. Just now I am indulging my femininity f. ex.

brittleness of Hydrocal forcedried by gas heat compared to hardness of HC not forcedried

Pieces suspected:

> Pecan pie
> Sundae
> Banana Split
> 3 (2) pies Javatime
> 2 candybars

My singleminded aim is to give existence to (my) fantasy. This means the creation of a parallel reality according to the rules of (my) fantasy.

I am compelled to do this to a greater degree than most painters.

This world cannot ever hope to really exist and so it exists entirely through illusion, but illusion is employed as subversively, as convincingly as possible.

The critical moment is my act of seeing. The rest is the patient reconstruction of this hallucination and successive hallucinations which arise in the course of making.

The contribution of subject matter is almost a side effect since what I see is not the thing itself but——myself——in its form.

Experience, that is to say, is material——for an act of recognition, and having recognized something, the job one could argue is done, the rest being the act of giving evidence.

Experience is the primary material & then plaster and paint. In the case of theater, experience is both the first and the second material.

The content is always the human imagination. This I regard both as historically constant and as universal among individuals. To present the geography of the human imagination is my aim, with real mountains and cities.

First Draft

STORE DAYS I

Period 1 : A Customer Enters.
Period 2 : A Bargain!
Period 3 : How The Founders Struggled.

Room 1: The BedRoom-Jail
Room 2: The Kitchen-ButcherShop
Room 3: The LivingRoom-Funeral Parlor-WhoreHouse

Feb. 12, 1962

Costume: bow tie, jacket, white shirt, pants. Pink feet.

Spirit: coral-pink party dress, $5 Orchard St. or 116th St. style with paper under to rustle and paper too in the hammock.

Hammock slit and black material, slit correspondingly, hung below.

On walls: pin-ups, statue of liberty, boxers, autos, in the manner of the basement room of the handy man at George Segal's farm.

A bed, very unmade. Dirty sheets, pillow. A bottle or two in bed. Comics. The floor covered with newspapers and clothing, and other debris from the street.

Lighting: bare bulbs frame scene, hurt eyes of spectators. To left a door and a hole, through which things will enter.

A chair, laden with clothes and objects. Pockets of jacket stuffed with various materials. Man unshaven.

Spirit makeup a la LES school girl, pancake white, white lips, darkened eyes, brows plucked in shape of chunky little birds, hair piled up etc or any variations of same.

As audience enters, spirit is rocking slowly above, the paper in her skirts and in the hammock rustling softly. The man sits on the edge of the bed with his socks in his hands. This is the *static tableau* or **position number 1.** It is held until the audience is settled or until more precisely end of first sub-period (2 mins).

Period 1: *The Sock*

The man drops his socks on the floor. A bell rings. A package is passed him from the opening in the left wall. He sits down and unwraps it. It is a pair of socks and a book and a can of tomato juice. What does he care? He lets it all drop on the floor.

He pulls the shade down between rooms 1 and 2 and lightning is projected on the shade. Sound of foghorns. He tosses on his bed. The spirit lowers a hand, dangles it. A leg, dangles it. The objects on the floor move. The ceiling sways.

end of period 1

Blue bulbs during positioning, always lit. 2 minutes of near-darkness. The man removes his coat and hangs it on the wall. He lies down and ties himself to the bed with one inch rope. He lies looking straight up. The hammock continues its gentle undulation.

A hard roll full of jam is dropped on the man's shirt from above. He frees one of his hands and eats it partly. From above and behind him (left wall) a pipe enters. Water runs out of it. He looks up at it. It goes away.

The floor moves (could be a person dressed as the floor). The leg protrudes down again. Milk is poured down around it. The man coughs violently. He ties himself tighter. The unfinished roll falls off his stained shirt. The radio goes on with distant sentimental music.

end of period 2

Position 3
The man takes off his shirt. Stands on the bed.

Period 3: *The Shoe*

The man kneels. He prays. His mouth moves. A glove is slipped in through the hole. He kisses it. Again——he shakes it. He gets on the floor on his knees, looking for his shoes under the bed. Everywhere.

The spirit drops coins, which fall on the floor . . . feathers . . . fruit . . . berries . . .

The man crawls under the bed. He emerges, his face covered with shaving cream. He sits down to put on his shoes, which he has found. The pipe returns, pouring water.

The spirit begins sliding down from the hammock through its center slit. Her skirt is caught above and we see her legs and underwear, then a rough cascade of newspapers, finally herself. She drops limply to the floor in a heap (to be a slow and beautiful action).

He coughs. He has one shoe on. He limps about looking for the other. He tears some pictures off the wall. He swears softly.

end of period 3
(and Store Days One, Room 1*)*

A kitchen-bathroom sink and stove. Tub and shower to right with hose from sink. Table in middle with two chairs and on it an elevatable top with created food. Another top with food under it. Perhaps a third. Stove is not operating. Oven stuffed with newspaper painted brown like fried chicken.

Two persons, man and woman. Woman dressed in T-shirt with a picture on it. The husband in a long underwear shirt. Woman at sink. Man at the table. A cutting board to her left full of vegetables and meat. An alcove full of groceries and meats in bags and structures which may in some simple way be made to fall down, above the sink. Sink full of dishes.

Above audience in "attic," operator Two, who is or is not same person as Room 2 spirit, a girl, nude, or so appearing, a cigarette advertisement type, a girl at the beach. Long hair and cigarette smoking. Her smoke fills the room, hangs like a cloud under the light on the action. Perhaps too, she burns incense or tar. She is made up with rosy cheeks and strong makeup. Long red nails, toes and fingers.

Position 1

The woman back to audience at sink full of dirty dishes. Man at table with dead cigar in hand. Spirit holds down a pack of cigarettes from attic, while smoking with other hand.

Period 1: *Dishes*

The woman turns. Mascara all over her face. However, she has not been crying. She appears jovial. One sees her tits through the T-shirt and her apron is wet. She wears a skirt with hearts all over it. She smiles in a frozen way, diagonally across the room at noone in particular.

The man sneezes and pushes all the dishes off the table with a swing of his arm. The table cloth is swept up and out by a wire. The spirit lowers a leg and wiggles her toes. The woman remains smiling. She takes a large cake from the alcove and pushes it into the man's face.

She bites a capsule in her mouth so that her mouth floods with what appears to be blood, which runs down her chin. The man falls over sideways. A sort of boring a terrible slapstick scene.

end of period 1

Position 2

The man returns to his seat. Sits slumped forward on the table in a plate of cold soup (which will to some extent wash off cake). Do not drown. The woman retains same position, smiling.

Period 2: *Conversation*

The woman comes to life with fast action begins chopping lettuce and other vegetables frantically. She brings down meat and chops it too frantically. She opens and closes stove, taking out brown newspapers and stuffing in food, taking out and stuffing in . . . Reaching up, she causes a great many things to fall down.

She attaches shower hose, runs to shower, wets herself, washes herself, with clothes on. Always smiling. The dishes fall off the sink with a great clatter.

Darkness. The spirits face descends upside down and smoking. Talking silently to someone. The man snores, sneezes in the soup.

end of period 2

Position 3

The spirits face swings back and forth in the semidarkness, humming in a high voice. The man wipes his face and sits up straight, reading a magazine. Talking silently pulls down shade over sink and sits down at the table opposite the man.

Period 3: *The Argument*

For two subperiods, slides are flashed on the screen. The man harrumphs. The woman whistles and belches.

Lights. She is eating ice cream with chocolate sauce. It drops on her stockings. She scrapes it off with her spoon but it gets away from her.

The pictures continue vaguely above the two.

The woman slams the ice cream down sloppily on the table spilling what is left out of the glass which overturns.

Darkness. More slides. The woman sneezes. She cries and laughs. She falls over backwards.

The man puts down magazine. He stands up before window between second and third room, stretches. He picks up a hammer, then a saw and saws furiously at a bench.

end of period 3
and STORE DAYS ONE, ROOM 2

A longer room. With three separately defined playing areas. The near: a couch perpendicular to audience and a closet door (door also to "outside"). Above door: a shelf big enough for a person, about 3 ft. high, 4 ft. wide . . . A "slide" beside the couch up to or down from the shelf. In center, a painted fireplace and mantelpiece loaded with objects. Above which, a mural of simple intention: trees, cows, a pretty girl or two. As in a bar or a restaurant. Substitute perhaps advertising photos in color, cut out and pasted.

The room is tangerine color, warm by contrast to the other two rooms which are black and white. It is "technicolor." The lighting is very bright but can be toned down to a simple shaded yellow bulb over a table and a chair in the center. Objects on table are quite important (as on kitchen table and floor of bedroom——stages themselves for small actions) . . . a blacked out statue of liberty, a cup, cards . . .

At far end a square area, on which opens a small hidden room (a toilet).

In this room Operator 3 and/or hidden figure. From this, a spotlight or bright light can be shot onto wall, illuminating square area.

This is a space for a family plot. To each area: daughter, father, mother. A shelf over the audience faces a mirror and there is the place of a third spirit, Room 3 spirit, a pinup.

Position I

Father is playing cards at table under yellow light. Daughter is at closet, pulling out clothes. The shelf above the closet is also full of clothes, all stuffed with paper. Mother is cutting material in the corner. Sound of her scissors in the darkness.

Period 1: *Death of Natural Causes*

Daughter pulling out clothes, pulling them down, an avalanche of bulging clothing, climbing up slide to reach them and pull them down frantically. They tumble down over her. One of them, her suitor, either in the closet or down from above. She throws him on the floor. He too is dressed in a stuffed suit, perhaps in womens clothes. The bottom of the closet is full of jewelry, pots and pans and other metallic objects, which daughter stirs with her feet. Her heels make a lot of noise. Her long hair swings this way and that. Dance music plays.

Mother laughs violently and walks the length of the mantelpiece and with a deliberate movement pushes down with her arm all the objects there. She stands at end, smiling victoriously. In the square space she left an inexplicable creature appears. She walks back, past her husband who is still playing cards. The creature is gone.

The father lays out all manner of peculiar sentimental and ridiculous objects on the table. He picks his nose from time to time.

end of period 1

Father the same. Daughter sits down on couch. Mother returns to her corner, sits down at sewing machine on table with her back to the room.

Period 2: *Making love after a date*

The mother knocks over the sewing machine and kicks it. The strange animal enters and goes out again.

The daughter takes off her clothes to her underwear. She pulls at her suitor tumbled among the clothing.

Someone, an apparition, a woman looks out of the closet door, very beautiful. She is gone. The daughter sits on the couch. She climbs up the slide. The apparition appears again. The suitor stands up and rubs his head ("Where am I?").

The mother is making a large drawing on the wall.

The father has donned a mask and is sitting without moving at all. The lights go out leaving him there with his mask on.

end of period 2

Position 3

Daughter on shelf sits dressing herself in another set of clothes. She puts on white stockings and white gown. She washes off her makeup in a pan of water.

Father raises up a structure and puts himself in it as a sort of body mask. A sphinx? He lies down on the floor.

Mother onto floor, she puts her ankle into a strap attached to a pulley.

Period 3: *The PhoneCall*

Daughter finishing her re-dressing and removing makeup slides down to the couch. Suitor is still lying amid debris. She uncovers a box of very greasy machinery and picks it out dirtying herself.

A drum roll then begins to play.

The mother is pulled across the floor by the enigma which secures her above the floor upside down and then enters. Dance music.

The enigma joins itself to the mask of the father. The apparition appears.

From the shelf above audience . . . a figure lowers itself down into the audience dispensing little pats of shaving cream and kisses. Mirrors spin.

The apparition smiles . . . a black tooth.

end of period 3
and STORE DAYS ONE, ROOM 3

sketch for a play

❋ R A Y   G U N   T H E A T E R ❋

Prod. C. Oldenburg

Schedule

Winter-Spring 1962

STORE DAYS	1st version	Feb. 23, 24
	2nd version	Mar. 2, 3
NEKROPOLIS	1st version	Mar. 9, 10
	2nd version	Mar. 16, 17

INJUN	1st version	Apr. 20, 21
	2nd version	Apr. 27, 28
VOYAGES	1st version	May 4, 5
	2nd version	May 11, 12
WORLD'S FAIR	1st version	May 18, 19
	2nd version	May 25, 26

No Theater between March 17 and April 20.

All performances in rear three rooms at Ray Gun Mfg. Co., 107 E. 2nd St. (between Ave. A and 1st Ave.), unless otherwise announced.

Audience limited by available space to 35 each night. Reservations necessary. Call OR4-0380 or GR5-4681, or write.

Performances start at 8:30 P.M.

over

❋ S T O R E D A Y S ❋

Cast

Version 1 :

Milet Andreyevich	Terry Brook
Billy Kluver	Letty Lou Eisenhauer
Jean Jacques Lebel	Gloria Graves❋
Claes Oldenburg❋	Mickey Henrion
Lucas Samaras❋	Johanna Lawrenson
	Pat Oldenburg❋
	~~Carol Lee Schneeman~~ CAROLEE SCHNEEMANN

Assisting:

Max & Anita Baker

Version 2 :

Henry Geldzahler	Rachel Drexler
Claes Oldenburg❋	Gloria Graves❋
Lucas Samaras❋	Pat Oldenburg❋
	Jackie Ferrara
	Charlotte Tokayer

and others...

Three ten-minute periods. Two pauses. No intermission.

❋ Repertory cast.

Budget for Theater

My theater activity in the coming season I would like to be in two manners. The first is a repertory type of theater, to give short performances at regular intervals, f.ex. every two weeks, on Saturdays 10 PM. These would be held in My Store, or The Ray-Gun Mfg Co., 107 E. 2nd St., N.Y.C. inside the store or in the courtyard behind the store, which is quite large. Since these performances would be comparatively brief, a small amount would be charged for admission, f.ex. 50¢, and the audience would have to be rather small. These performances would occur one time only and be improvised out of available material and available performers, with no great expense. There would not need to be any advertising, I think. In fact, advertising might bring too many people. It is better to be word of mouth. This repertory would be like a workshop of ideas and possibilities surrounding my concept of personal theater, and not so much directed at the general public as at other artists and connoisseurs interested in developments along this line. On the basis of one performance every two wks. and starting in October, there would be about 14 performances. Assuming about 35 spectators can be accommodated, there would be an income of $17.50 per performance. A supplementary budget of $25 would be needed for each performance, or for 14 perfs——$350.

8

The store an efflorescence additive principle clusters agglomerations magnetic attractions extension flaming chairs and tables outrushing pictures on the wall moveables all moving earthquake   Torn-birth flesh-fragments. I think of space as material as I think of the stage as a solid cube or a box to be broken. That air and the things in it are one, are HARD, and that you can RIP a piece of air and the thing out of it, so that a piece of object and a whole object and just air, comes as one piece. This is accompanied by a RIPPING SOUND

The starting point of the realist is to be the scientist. Nature *means* nothing by itself. Man supplies the meaning of things. My theatre, which may be called the theatre of the real or the theatre of the object, is a meeting place of realistic and subjective nature whose sentimental representation is juxtaposed with non-sentimental.

A theater of action or of things (people too regarded as things).

but above all, am i worth coming to see? it is a poor man's theatre and the lead is a beggar.

A series of plays dealing with the US consciousness, really nonconcrete in content though expressed concretely. The content is the US mind or the US "Store". This is not understood. Despite what I say, the pieces are called happenings. I might have done happenings or may do in the future but these are not my idea of them. RG is something else, closely related to my Store pieces. It seeks to present in events what the store presents in objects. It is a theater of real events (a newsreel) . . . Have shorts?

Giving hair and muscles and skin to thoughts

Nothing is communicated or represented except through its attachment to an object (even though the object will mean different things at the same moment to different people) . . . It is the play of consciousness in reaction to certain objects . . . a play which involves the consciousness of myself my actors and my audience . . . This differs from conventional theater in that the communication is less fixed . . . more in doubt . . . there is a sequence but not plot or given relation of the events and objects as they occur . . . the sequence is purely a practical device . . . plot to me is sentimentality, pre-determination, an arrogance on the part of an author, a harmful fabrication which creates a residue of sentimental patterns that keep men from per-ceiving experience . . . this theater aims to make man compose experience as it changes a constant pleasure and an instrument of survival . . .

Who is the bum the Rag Man of my dreams

The theater differs from the store in that the objects of the store are reproductions, reconstructions or alterations of the actual object. This is also an anti neorealist expression. I have tried to represent my consciousness in relation to the actual object at the moment of my perception of it. This is complicated by the facts of construction . . . and there is only one way to handle this: to treat the materials as a complicating factor of the object, themselves objects of consciousness. On top of this I have complicated the object by introducing conventions of popular representation and artistic practise (a sort of travesty). The object is a record of passage through these complications . . . and must be seen as itself and not in relation to any theory. The aim of putting the store in an actual neighborhood is to *con-trast* it to the actual object . . . not as might be thought in neorealist terms to point up similarities . . . The store title is in fact a play on words . . . the store means for me: my consciousness. . . .

In the store then, the work is as if done for the spectator whereas in RG theater, using actual objects (though affected by situation) . . . the spectator has more latitude in perception . . . actually there is always this latitude even in relation to the prepared object . . .

my characters are the city-bird-child (chick) and the beggar. innocence and experience. that is my theme: innocence vs. experience (or evil).
good vs. evil. comic innocence. pat.

Farce for Objects, in a bright light . . .

A black and white (upholstered) white convertible
Gold shoes
Water (in the gutter)
An iron . . . in the sun

I am very grateful to the audience for coming each weekend. I cannot
deny it is good to have an audience, though the nature of this theater is such
that it would go on without an audience as a painter might go on painting
with noone to watch him . . . This space has great limitations, I am aware of
this . . . partly I enjoy the pressure these limitations put on me . . . I mean
the time, the expense and the space . . . I hope you are not too miserable
. . . my aim is to develop under these concentrated circumstances a sort of
kernel of infinite expansion . . . so that at the end of this season I shall have
ten extremely powerful seeds . . . It is becoming obvious I guess that these
pieces are not unrelated . . . the "happening" which was in the beginning a
very limited form is bearing fruit as a new physical theater, bringing to the
dry puritan forms of the US stage the possibilities of a tremendous envelop-
ing force . . .
Theater is the most powerful art form there is because it is the most
involving . . . but it is forever becoming lost in trivialities . . . loss of power is
a chronic disease of the form . . . realism . . . distance . . . commercial pres-
sures . . . poor theater . . . I no longer see the distinction between theater and
visual arts very clearly . . . distinctions I suppose are a civilized disease . . .
I see primarily the need to reflect life . . . to give back, which is the only
activity that gives man dignity . . . I am especially concerned with physicality, which is evident . . . only painting and sculpture have the power to
give man back his physicality (which is not primitivism) when he loses
it . . . painting and sculpture have the unique privilege of affecting the other
arts in this respect . . .

STORE DAYS I

Feb. 23–24   1962

3 periods——3 rooms
2 pauses
no intermission

Cast

ROOM I	spirit man
ROOM II	spirit man woman
ROOM III	spirit woman 1 woman 2 two men a man and a woman
OPERATORS	Lighting——one Objects——one, near station

Total 13

——Five main stations of lights   15 watt white
              15 watt white
               5 watt blue
              15 watt white
              25 watt yellow
——Three 5 watt color lights on throughout, one in each room.
  near floor in first room
——Extra——15 watt hammock light and in far station (toilet)
——Eccentrics——none

Lighting Instructions and other instructions

 3 periods of 10 minutes each——2 pauses.
 Each 10 min. period divided into 2½ main periods——one length of 5 stations at 30 seconds each.
 Stations are changed every 30 seconds in sequence 1–2–3–4–5 1–2–3–4–5 etc.
 Pause between 10 min. periods of 30 seconds.
 Lights cue action (at station) which freezes when light leaves for adjoining station
 Total time 31 min.
 Action thus for each station 6 min total out of 30.
 Script (by individual performers, operator) identifies piece, room, station treated, activity, partners, on same page.
 Performers action is described by 30 second periods, in three parts:

	a	opening action
1.	b	middle, combined action, or development
	c	closing action

Closing action of one 30 sec. period is same as opening action of next

x

 Spirits operate freely outside mechanical scheme improvising with certain effects in dark and light periods

Audience is limited to 35. A bench or platform along wall——two rows——separated from the action by a clothesline in each room. The effect of a sideshow, or historical rooms. The audience stands, backs to the wall. Can move to take in all rooms. After performance are led out by Operator I either thru side door or where they came thru store.

x

Dressing room outside near end of rooms.

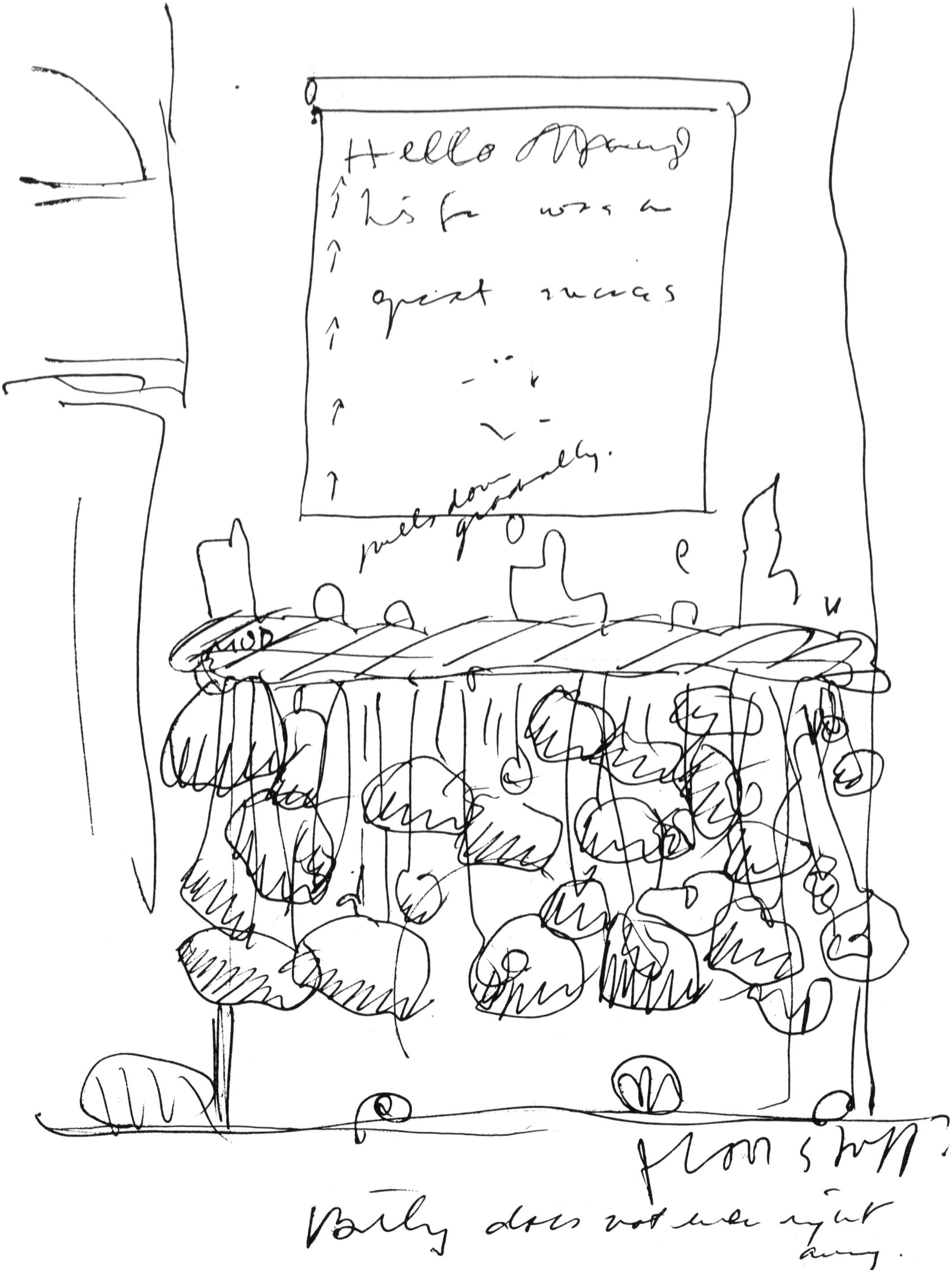

Hello
pulls down gradually.

Action takes place in 3 rooms in a line between which are large open windows, so that one can see easily from one room to the other. The smallest room, Room I, is designated the BEDROOM. Room II, a bit larger, has a sink & is the KITCHEN. Room III, has a fireplace & mantelpiece & is called the LIVING ROOM. Off from III is a small toilet used for exits & entrances & by Operator II, if needed. Operator I & lighting man are stationed outside Room I. Thru a slot lighting man can see all 3 rooms.

An ATTIC is built over half of Room II above the audience and extending thru doors into Room I & II. A door leads out into a corridor from Room II.

ROOM I: DESCRIPTION

The smallest room. painted all black. the floor is covered with debris, recollections, trash of a historical nature, carefully selected. wood pieces, photos, newspaper clippings, paper, cloth, chairs, rope, comic books, books to improve oneself, candy wrappers, cans, cartons, bottles, packages, food remnants, notes, letters, shoes and other articles of clothing etc. etc.

Furniture: a bench which serves as a bed on which a mattress of unbleached muslin stuffed with newspapers. All soiled and the bed also littered with debris.

A chair over which a muslin cover to which is sewn more debris, mostly clothing—pants, ties, keys, buttons, flowers, wallets, glasses, handkerchiefs, old tickets, socks, money, etc. etc.

In a corner a smashed radio, labeled "automatic"

Pasted on the wall are cut out reproductions of pin-ups, automobiles

ROOM I: MAN

Station 1
Description, costume & general position
A THIN MAN.
Costume: a dark jacket, a yellowed shirt with a starched curled up collar. A striped clip on bow tie. Underwear, striped shorts. No pants. Bare feet, painted pink.

The pockets of his jacket stuffed w. objects, trivia, debris.

x

He sits, kneels, lies on the bed, crawls under it, walks around the room (which has the appearance of a cave or a jail cell).

Description, costume and general positions

A YOUNG WOMAN, medium height or small.

Costume: Organdy dress with full skirt——brilliant yellow color. Silk stockings,

Position: lying in hammock & rocking. Hammock is filled w. newspaper which rustles. The skirt of dress is also filled w. newspaper.

On a shelf for the spirits use, a number of effects & objects, as indicated.

A private light. Access to "attic"

Room II

A room slightly larger than Room I. Also painted black with the relief of a few cut-outs, mostly of reproductions of food from magazines. A piece in the form of a painting like a dressing table with a shelf on which a cracked mirror, a womans head from a postcard, a large smudged postcard of the Empire State building, fragments of makeup.

At R. a sink and a cutting board. A hose leads from the faucet over the window to a point at the end of the cutting board where the water spouts out into a pan. On the cutting board a cleaver, some slashed vegetables (red cabbage, yams, sweet potatoes, f. ex). On the ledge above, between Room I & 2, some blue cloth flowers in a bottle, shaving cream, Lavoris, a prescription bottle etc.

Above the sink, an alcove, over which, a white shade, half lowered, to catch projections of Spirit II in attic. Full of painted paper bags of all kinds stuffed with paper and various debris arranged to fall down easily.

To left several bundles of firewood, an axe, a saw.

A trumpet hanging on wall and an unfinished ship model.

Furniture: A table and two chairs. The table has a top of stuffed muslin on which plates, cups, silver and food debris is sewn or otherwise attached (glued, stuck in, plastic). Under this stuffed top another and under that still another, all like pillows (or pancakes).

Room II   Man and Woman

Station 2

Description, costume & general position

Woman: Blond, "plump".

Man: "stocky".

Costumes: woman wears T-shirt on which something is printed in several colors and an ordinary white skirt with pink hearts printed on it. Short socks.

Man: long-underwear top & pants.

Generally at ease in kitchen.

Woman at sink, cutting board and table to Right.

Man seated & moving around to left.

Room II Spirit II

Description, costume and general position

Short, long-hair girl

Costume:

General position: in "attic" over room

Room III

A longer room than the other two and painted tangerine color. The window between Room II & III is taller and the sill of it forms a seat on which is a cushion of muslin, painted & stuffed & lined with dangling many-colored strips of cloth.

Next to the seat a closet w. two doors, full of womens clothes stuffed w. newspaper. Inside of closet painted yellow & blue like a landscape. On the floor of the closet a collection of cans & other metal & glass & paper objects (bottles, caps, lids etc. etc.) sprayed aluminum color to a depth of about 2 feet. The doors to the closet are shut when piece begins.

Above closet, an alcove, lined w. puffed-up stuffed painted muslin, decorative, position of Spirit III.

Below & in center is a raised small stage about 2 feet by 4 feet built over the mantelpiece of a fireplace and a wooden "horse".

Below this stage is an area enclosed by painted muslin with a slit in front. Behind the raised stage the wall is decorated with cut-outs from magazines, photostats and certain objects hung on the wall.

To the left, a tall square area, beyond the raised stage (the ceilings are high), a tall paneless window in which a pulley and rope attached to a belt. A bench perpendicular to window, against wall.

(develop more)

Room III Spirit III

Description, costume, general position

Blackhaired woman.

Costume: All white, layers of abundant white material, like a bride, long skirt, half-circle headdress of white.

Mirrors or spangles in hair. Small flashlights in costume. Features intensified by makeup.

General position: seated facing R. face turned toward audience.

Room III   Woman 2

Station 4

Description, costume, general position

Tall, slender, long legs, good figure, dark.

Costume: Adhesive tape on face. The type of a 3rd Ave. wanderer, perhaps a gypsy. Dress, silk stockings, high heels, ankle jewelry. Added long black hair. Bizarre makeup. Purse w. objects as described: knife, coins, flowers etc.

General position: walking sitting kneeling on raised stage, (showing) or in other ways using wall.

Room III   Two Men

Station 4

Description, Costume & gen'l position

1. Short, "stocky". Beggar. In bizarre burlap costume, carrying bundles of newspapers and a traveling bag full of objects, and a sandwich in a wrapper.

2. Long, "stocky"——wrapped in paper and tied with twine.

---

1. Sitting in front of, below raised stage—the lower "street".

2. Protruding slightly from the muslin which hangs from raised stage. To be pulled out.

Inside & under raised stage——a bass drum, played by the packageman.

Room III   Man & Woman

Station 5

Description, Costume, general position

Man——slender, tall.

Costume: baggy ordinary coat & hat. Pockets stuffed with objects. Jockstrap under.

Woman——slender tall. polka dot dress——silk stockings. Heels. Everyday costume.

G.P. Man——in & out of room (into toilet)——up on bench. Woman——around area of station.

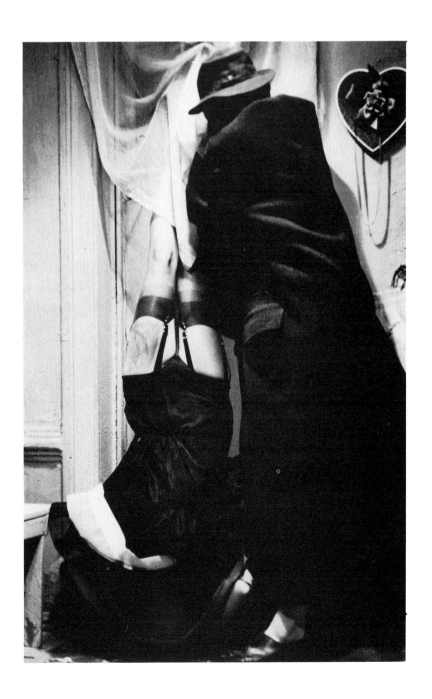

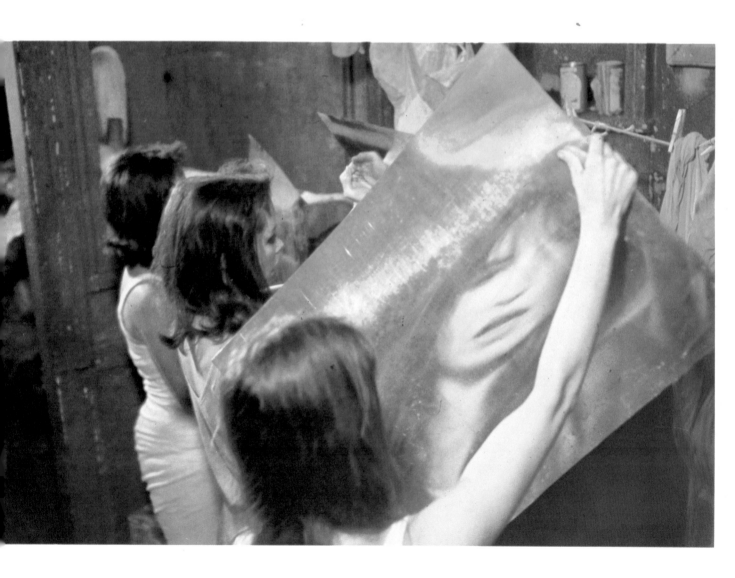

9

Room I
(Man, Spirit, Operator of Object Effects)

Man	Spirit	Objects
12 events	1 cue	3 cues
With socks	Free:	
1 Drops socks	Rocks,	1 Bell Rings
Gets package	Rustles	Hands package
	Dangles head,	
Gets Package	Limbs	
2 Opens Package	Milk on Leg	
Drops Package	On Head, Arm	
	Drops Coins	Free:
Drops Package	(spread	Projects
3 Lies Down	thruout)	Megaphones
Tosses		Gravity Band
		Floor Moves
Tosses		Pipe Enters (2)
4 Takes off Coat		Radio
Roll Drops	Drop Roll	(spread
		thruout)

Man	Spirit	Objects
Roll Drops		
5 Eats Roll		
Leaves Roll		
(lies w. roll)		
Lies with Roll		
6 Takes off Shirt		
Kneels on Bed		
Kneels on Bed		7 Sticks in Glove
7 Kisses Glove		
Shakes Glove		
Shakes Glove		
8 Looks for Shoe		
Looks for Shoe		

Man	Spirit	Objects
Looks for Shoe		
9 Finds Shoe		
Puts on Shoe		

Puts on Shoe
10   Into a Rage
Runs around
  Swears, Tears

Runs around, etc.
11   Lies Down
Ties Himself to Bed

Ties Himself to Bed
12   Ties Himself to Bed
Ties Himself to Bed
  (coughs)

Slides Down

ROOM II, STATION 2
(MAN, WOMAN)

Period I.: Dishes

Woman

1. Drying dishes
   Stacks them above   drinks water
        smiles   mascara runs
   Same

2. Takes pie out of plastic container
   Picks at it   sobs
   Pushes it into man's face
        impulsively
        laughs

3. Laughs
   Unwraps ice cream bar
   Eats it

4. Eats bar, leaves it half eaten
        it falls on floor
   Pulls at tooth   mouth fills w.
        blood, wipes it
   Laughs, looks for ice cream bar but
        its fallen down

Man

1. Carving ship model
   Examines it   carves
   Sands it

2. Sanding
   Sudden Anger, grabs up table
        and crumples it
        throws it down
   Sits down   gets pie in face

3. Wipes pie off face
        with second table top
   Picks up first
        sets everything right
   Takes up magazine

4. With shears cuts pinup
        from magazine
   same
   Pastes it up on wall with tape

Period II. Soup

1. Wipes mouth
   Turns on water (before)
   Washes hair

2. Goes to alcove   hair wet
        wringing it   gets soup plate
   Pours soup (from under table)
   Sets before him
   Goes back to hair

1. Sits down and lites cigar
   Takes up trumpet
   Smokes now plays now

2. Smokes & plays
   Gets soup
   Smokes plays sucks soup

3. Dries hair
   Talks to self, ignores him
   Gets cup of ice cream   sits down
       at table

3. Knocks soup off it tastes
       terrible
   Takes up ship model   carves
       on it   a little spite
   Throws model at her

4. Drops ice cream on thighs   tries
       to get it back in but cant
   Slams glass on table, coughs
   Lights cigarette and talks to self

4. Bundles up table again
       in rage
   Throws down first, second
       third piece
   Looks for ship model

Period III: Vegetables

1. Takes down vegetables from above
       sink
   Chops wildly plantains, cabbages,
       roots etc.
   Chops chops

1. Picks up the three table tops
       and lays them on again
   Picks up pieces of soupplate
   Touches pinup
   Sets out shaving stuff

2. Chops
   Looking for something causes all the
       bags and stuff above sink and
       dishes to fall down
   Indifferent, chops away

2. Lathers his face and starts to
       shave
   Curses woman and throws shaving
       cream at her
   Pushes table aside and still
       wearing cream picks up wood

3. Throws chopped stuff in water
       stirs   sits down at table
       (as if waiting for it to cook)
   Pours drink from bottle   whistles
   Peels potatoes   scratches hair
       cries a little

3. Unties wood and starts to chop it
   Saws it
   Looks for ship model

4. Falls asleep, drops potato
   Snores   sags off chair
   Wakes up sort of but not much

4. Looks for ship model
   Finds it
   Throws it down angrily
   Chops
   Saws

Room III, station 3
Woman 1

Period I: ToeNails

1. Sits on couch
   Gets up walks
   Walks in a circle fast on
     hard floor clicking

2. Still walking
   Sits down curls up slowly
   Looks at body, turns legs
     looks at legs   drops off shoes

3. Still looking
   Abruptly rolls down stockings &
     off drops
   Begins cutting toenails with
     great care and pleasure

4. Still cutting
   Gets up walks around abruptly
     one stocking off one on
   Sits down again

Period II: Letters

1. Takes hand mirror off wall
   Practises smiling
   Sets mirror back, curls around

2. Loosens hair
   Takes mirror again, practises funny
     faces and terrible ones
   Curls, hangs mirror back

3. Stretches
   Takes off eyelashes   takes envelope
     out of pocket   puts them in, puts
     under couch

4. Curls, takes letters out from under
     couch
   Reads them all very fast   white,
     pink, blue black green
   Cries laughs tears them all up and
     falls asleep

Period III: The Closet

1. Spits off couch
   Puts legs up high falls off
   Stands up starts undressing

2. Takes off clothes
   Walks around
   Abruptly, opens closet doors

3. Pulls out all clothes angrily
   Kicks them around
   Kicks them around

4. Squats pulls out all stuff at bottom
     shoes and silvered cans etc.
     much clatter
   Just walks around

ROOM III, STATION 4
Woman 2
(on raised stage in walking position)

Period I: The Banana

1. Just strolls, back and forth
     swinging bag, taps, smiles, smokes
   Just strolls back and forth
     swinging bag taps smiles
   Stops, looks in purse

2. Looks in purse
   Takes out banana, peels eats, while
     smoking

3. Takes newspaper out from under arm
   Reads paper, swears, looks at watch
     throws hair back
   Dances with paper in front of face,
     slaps it, argues with it

4. Dances, folds paper messily   throws
     down. Walks fast, worried
   Hesitation. draws on gloves
   Draws on gloves looks around nervously

Period II: The Knife

1. Takes off gloves glances around walks
   Puts gloves in pocket kicks paper
   Opens purse, spills coins down on Milet

2. Kneels to get coins, forgets them
   Examines pieces of paper
   Stands up stamps out cigarettes

3. Takes knife out of purse flips it
   Stabs wall several times
   Ouch, cuts herself

4. Sucks wound
   Pares nails with knife, cries
   Dries tears with back of hand
     bites lips
   Walks

Period III: The Umbrella

1. Walks grabs camera
   Takes pictures this way and that
   Symmetrizes skirt, drops camera
   Takes out makeup and mirror, fixes face

2. Walks, picks flowers out of bag
and sticks them roughly in hair
Walks on, scratching

3. Stamps around, swears
Hums, taps
Looks behind her hums taps

4. Grabs umbrella puts up suddenly, smiles
Flirts from under umbrella
Becomes serious
Red paint runs down walls

Room III, station 4
Two Men

Period I: The Sandwich

One

1. In package
   In package   (plays drum)
   In package

2. In package
   In package   (plays drum)
   In package

3. As above

4. As above

Two

1. Emerges from under stage
   with newspaper bundles
   and bag and sandwich
   Same
   Same

2. Comes round front, sets
   stuff down
   Sits
   Eats sandwich, wrapped in map
   (banana peel comes down)

3. Swears to woman
   Eats sandwich
   Blows nose swears eats
   sandwich   plans trip on map

4. Sees package
   Feels it   pulls it out
   Begins to unwrap it

Period II: The Package

1. As above but is unwrapped
   Is pulled out

2. As above

3. As above

4. As above

1. Unwraps package
   Unwraps package to shoes
   To legs

2. Up legs
   Up legs
   Middle

3. Eats sandwich
   Stomach unwrapped, tie
   Goes thru pockets

4. Chest unwrapped
   Goes thru chest pockets
   Nothing, loses interest
   Eats sandwich

Period III: The Handbag

1. Wrapped again
     carelessly stuffed back

2. Same   once back in resumes
   drum

3. Same

4. Same

1. Wraps carelessly up
   Stuffs package back
   Stuffs back and wraps

2. Finishes sandwich goes back
     to map
   Takes out bag and opens it
   Spreads bag

3. Takes objects out of bag
   Takes objects out of bag
   Takes objects out of bag

4. Looking for something
   Takes objects out of bag
   Finds knife, kisses   runs
     along cheek

Coordinated: none

Improvised:

I. shows black shiny pistol
raises leg   lowers other
wiggles toes
handghost (runs cloth thru
    fingers)

use all thruout—
more coming

II. shoots caps
fans self

III. bells
handcymbals

Room III, station 5
Man and Woman

Period I: Pockets

Man

1. Man enters
Goes thru pockets frantically
Goes thru pockets frantically

2. Goes thru pockets frantically
Kisses her
Hits her

3. Lights cigarettes
Drops objects out of pockets
    some on floor, on bench, to her

4. Refuses pig
Smashes the pig
Goes back to looking thru pockets

Woman

1. Seated on bench with
    ceramic pig
Stands up
Helps him look

2. Hits him
Hits him
Phone rings, she answers it

3. Talks on phone
Gives him pig to hold
Insists he hold pig

4. Insists he hold pig
Indifferent. Talks on phone
Puts phone down

Period II: Clay

1. Takes off coat
Gets up on bench
Strikes pose

2. Poses
Puts bag over face
Poses

3. Poses with bag on head
Poses with bag on head
Poses with bag on head

4. Puts on coat takes off bag
Leaves
Off

1. Takes out clay
Drops clay
Drops clay leaves it

2. Takes up pencil & pipe
Draws
Draws

3. Turns bag
Turns it again
Ignores subject drops paper

4. Pick up greasy machine parts
Examines them
Examines, takes out.

Period III: Haircut

1. Off
Returns
Sits on bench lites cigarette
   talks fast

2. Sits on bench lites cigarette
   talks fast
Turns around sits facing wall
Brings out more objects

3. Looking in pockets
Looking in pockets
Gets wig and cuts

4. Gets up grabs her violently
   forces her to floor
Puts legs in sling
Pulls her up

1. Sits down with greasy fingers
Draws, erases
Drops paper, talks fast

2. Talks fast
Crosses legs back and forth
Makes little notes on stocking

3. Stands up brushes skirt
   vigorously
Grabs scissors, snips in air
Throws wig on him & cuts it
   throws wig on self & cuts it

4. Lies down talking fast
   no resistance
Is pulled up
Is pulled up

end

Residual Objects

Love objects. respect objects.

Objectivity high state of feeling.

Residual objects are created in the course of making the performance and during the repeated performances. The performance
is the main thing but when it is over there are a number of sub-
ordinate pieces which may be isolated, souvenirs, residual objects.

To pick up after a performance to be very careful about what is
to be discarded and what still survives by itself. Slow study
& respect for small things. Ones own created "found objects"
The floor of the stage like the street. Picking up after is
creative. Also their partifular life must be respected. where
they had their place, each area of activity combed separately
and with respect for where it begins & ends.

Residual Objects, Store Days 1.

Room 1.

The Chair

The Bed (incomplete)

A fragment of the floor.   various small objects

popular graphics   wood

Room II.

The table, in three parts

The wall-piece   various small objects

Wood

Magazines -

Container of sliced vegetables-

Room III

a.

A closet-full or table full of ~~stuffed~~ dresses & other *[handwritten]*
    clothing *[handwritten notes]*
    [handwritten]

Packet of pink letters on a settee *[handwritten]*

Two cases of silvered ~~free~~ cans ~~and~~ bottles *[handwritten]*
    [handwritten] containers

b. *[handwritten: black decorated with colored ... representing ...]*

Wall and street-plain (on which a black umbrella
    spattered with white pai~~n~~t, flowers, coins, other
    street debris.
    [handwritten: crusted w. concrete ...]

Altar of construction horse/~~with~~ cardboard bo~~e~~xs full of
    nails and painted black ~~tied under it.~~
    [handwritten: corduroy pants]

Half a man in blue socks and plasterspattered shoes tied in
    furniture-wrapping paper, ripped and leaking gray matter,
    ~~with~~ nailed wood and other debris
    [handwritten: tied w. twine / tied w. twine]

A ~~bag~~ full of debris and various objects ~~and~~ newspaper bundles

~~various other objects~~ ~~& costumes~~

c.

A box of objec~~te~~s *[handwritten notes in margin and right]*

A ~~plastic~~ pail of ~~brown~~ mud

A box of machinery ~~greasy~~

A bag of newspaper strips

A pad of yellow paper with ~~marks and grease on it~~
    {drawings}

A telephone.

*[handwritten: Bag w. 2 faces drawn on it.
Chocolate box in shape of head ... cloth ...]*

Costumes

Certain p rticular costumes, to be photographed as objects

Shirt and shorts and clip on bow tie~~s~~
    [handwritten: staff yellowed striped]

Terrys *[handwritten]* . *[handwritten: black stocking ...]*

Carolees	Milets	Billys coat and hat	Lettys	Mickeys
[spotted dress, blue stockings]	*[striped, baggy pants w. twine]*	*grea[t] overcoat, work shop, brown ... hat, belt burlap + muslin coat*	*[pink dress, black/red ...]*	*bridal gown*

STICK WITH LEPAGE'S

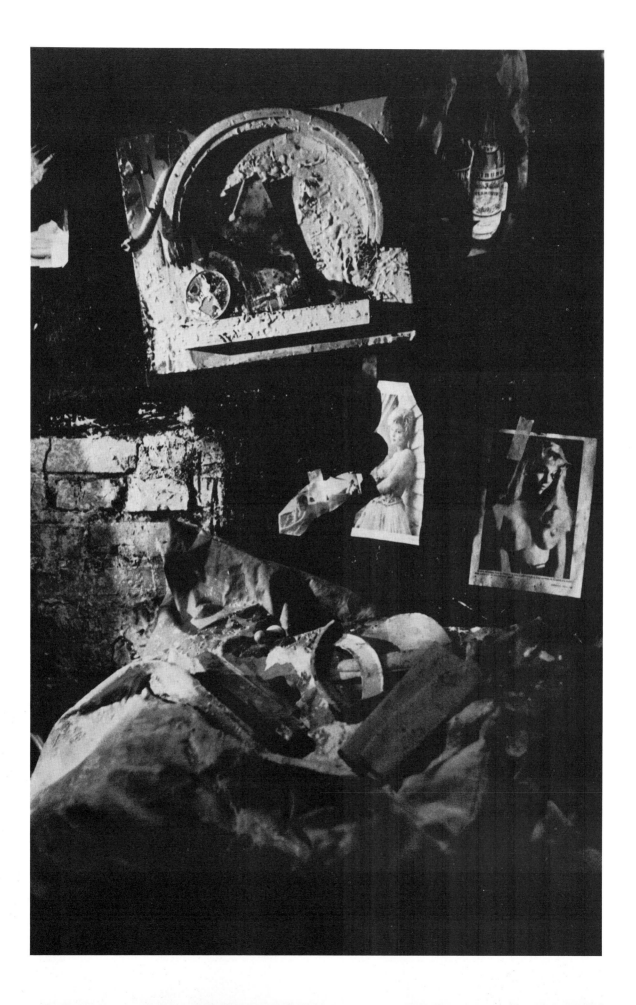

great ugly unresolved chinks and fragments....of despair and

impotence and frustration....from emptiness at first now to

positive despair...

the form and technique does serve a meaning intention, I really

cant deny it.. no escape, resolution...dark ugly stuff..

boredom or violence...

hideous picture of life...

store--bore

mans indoor life in winter
store days showed desperation and boredom of gayety

Nekropolis showed the kingdom of impotence and death
underground life
Injun shows the kingdom of instinctive violence (in Dallas

combined with desperation, impotence and boredom and

death).   birth,.xxkxxxkxxx

The reas n for doing a series, and for cycles.. self discovery

or discovery of changes in self in relation to seasons and chg

circumstances...

With Injun I mean to be on the treshold of affirmation, breakthru

thru violence.. into beauty (Voyages) and Love (WF)

The violence in Injun should not be futile, as the butcher's of

Store Days

an element of resolution or ransformation is introduced...

finales of Injun is the unrolling of the cunt

First Draft

STORE DAYS II

Period 1: Something Purchased
Period 2: A Lecture to the Salesmen
Period 3: The Night Before Christmas

Room 1: BedRoom-Jail
Room 2: Kitchen-Butcher Shop
Room 3: LivingRoom-TurkishBath-WhoreHouse -Funeral Parlor

Position 1

In a room with dark walls, a great illuminated silver dressing table with mirrors
on all the walls around. Above in hammock a man, slight and handsome, with a trumpet. To side, a seat or sofa. Throughout, soft blinking lights.

A woman is seated at the mirror combing her hair, which is very long. On the
dresser, all manner of peculiar created objects.

Period 1: *Glass*

The woman turns on a fan standing on the table, which blows her hair.
"Whooooey!" she says, turning her head back and forth. It causes the wall opposite,
which is hung with plastic, to ripple and sway. The man above (the spirit) sticks his
head out of the hammock and blows his trumpet softly.

A man with his hair slicked down enters the room from left with a snare drum
in his hand which he sets down and a stool which he sets down and sits on. He takes
out sticks (or brushes). He begins to play politely and quietly, smiling at the audience. His hair is slicked down and he is all around a slick fellow.

The woman at the mirror looks at herself and makes up.

Another woman all in black and shrouded with a bulky black shroud enters and
walks back and forth between the audience and the others. She kneels down at right
and from a drawer takes out a pile of jewelry some of which she drops, some puts
on her.

The woman at the table turns on the fan again and goes "whooooey!" She stands
up abruptly and joins the other woman in front of the window between rooms one
and two. She draws down the shade (or butcher does). Photos of high mountains
are flashed on the shade and over them, one after another while they giggle and talk
rapidly animatedly intimately. The shrouded woman's face can barely be seen.

end of period one

Position 2

The shrouded woman removes her shroud and sits facing the audience on the
dressing table. The other woman resumes her seat facing the mirror. The woman in
black is made up grotesquely we now see. Her front teeth are gold. They flash when
she speaks.

Period 2: *Dreams*

The woman in black talks sidelong, charmingly, to the other woman who rather

21 ignores her, combing her hair. The woman in black slaps the other in the head. The other pays no attention.

The woman in black fans herself with a hand fan or a newspaper, crosses her legs, looks away.

The mans leg emerges with a handsome brown and white shoe, swaying. It goes back up comes down with a fine patentleather shoe.

The woman in black takes off her jewelry and throws it down, shakes her hair. She leans back and falls asleep instantly. She rolls gently off the table on the floor in the corner, where she stays until end.

Several letters are handed down to the woman combing her hair, some dropped aimlessly. She turns on the fan again and says "Whoooooey!" The drummer plays on, ingratiatingly.

end of period two

Position 3

Same, but drummer plays very slowly, not audibly and bass drum off stage makes the sound. His eyes are closed.

Period 3: *The Violin*

The first woman tucks her skirts up and ties flashlights on her legs above the knees, which dangle as she walks back and forth.

A reddish powder falls around the room.

A huge form begins to force its way into the room through the narrow door on the left, a sort of smiling face which expands, develops dimension inside the room.

The woman does not care. It expands until it literally fills the room, pushing the drummer and his drum aside. He falls over in fact.

The girl lies down on the seat at right with her book to the apparition.

She turns off the flashlights fastened to her legs and appears to go to sleep.

The apparition fills the whole room, and may by a hand pinch and write on her exposed legs.

end of period three
and end of
Store Days II, Room 1

Position One
A long table in the room and that is all. A sink. From walls and from ceiling, meats of all kinds, simulated, substituted, f.ex. paper forms, metal forms, deflated balls, white fuzzy muffs, nuts, bolts. Plastic bags of colored liquids, which may be cut. From above, also a string of meats hung before the eyes of the audience. Noone is in the room but the objects.

Upstairs, a spirit, male, with a striped shirt.

Period 1: *Rabbits*

Descending slowly from the attic, a winged butcher, with rimless glasses and in his hand a large cleaver which shines in the light. He slowly descends amid the undulating meats etc. in the room.

Puts down cleaver. Washes his hands and combs his hair in a mirror.

He lathers his face and begins to shave. Flashbulbs go off, blinding the audience (the spirit holds them down).

The butcher sings. A hand or a leg hangs down from time to time while the butcher shaves.

end of period one

Position Two
Same. Butcher goes on shaving. Finishes in the darkness. A film goes on of swimmers competing furiously and run at fast speed on the shade above the sink.

Period 2: *Wristwatches*

When light is on, he leaves off shaving abruptly, with cream still on his face. He begins taking objects down from the wall and smashing & vigorously beating them and chopping them, all sorts of objects. The spirit continues to dangle parts of anatomy from balcony. He throws a fine snow from time to time, through the cracks over the audience and into the room. He peers upside down at the audience inanely and tries to distract them.

The phone rings. The butcher answers, the phone drips blood. The mouthpiece is bloody. He is bothered by the call. After all he is busy. The blood smears on his lips.

end of period two

Position 3

The film of swimmers in darkness, at slow speed. The butcher remains standing at the phone. Sound of turning newspapers from above. Coughing and sneezing.

Period 3: *Virtuosity*

A package lands on the sitting room table thrown from above. The phone rings. Another package falls, lands. Some sausages. A rabbit. The butcher puts down the phone and wipes his mouth. He paces back & forth humming.

More packages are thrown down.

The butcher goes back to shaving. The mirror reflects the spirit.

Darkness. The film of swimmers.

The butcher shaves.

Sound of a violin and cashregisters.

The butcher droops his wings (they are on suspenders). He sits down at the table crying.

All the suspended objects drop on him and around him.

end of period three
and of STORE DAYS II, ROOM 2

Position 1

Organ music. In the closet, dark. Light goes on. In far corner, a tall Statue of Liberty on rollers—a real person in combine. In hidden room (toilet) an elephant. Three women seated on shelf over closet, legs dangling over side (the McGuire Sisters).

On mantelpiece a ship model which can be cranked up. In the sky: "clouds"—cloth bags around weak light bulbs which can be moved. On shelf above audience an operator with squirt guns of colored liquid. In far corner, a sort of band: a saxophonist and a singer in evening dress (or a Puerto Rican Bible band), smiling, next to statue.

The women seated on the shelf above the closet are dressed very lushly in bouffant skirts and made up with dark makeup which makes them look tanned. Their shoes glisten. Under their skirts hang pocket flashlites which illuminate their legs.

The length of the room is a shallow trough about 3 ft. by 9 ft. with about two inches of water in it, a sort of liquid dance floor or a plane runway after rainstorm. A hose at the left end which slowly pours water into the trough.

On the mantelpiece is a sign also, a box with simulated neon letters which reads "Hot Dogs."

Period 1: *Baldness*

A man in evening suit and a derby enters. The President of the U.S. handsome slick. He goes to mantle, hangs up his hat, turns on Hot Dog sign. The clouds move back and forth. (A moon hangs down)

Sound of cashregisters. The girls sitting on the shelf hum and move their legs in time to the rhythm. The saxophonist plays.

The Statue of Liberty moves a little.

The gentleman takes out a mirror and breaks it with his hands. Then another—from all his pockets. He coughs, smiles.

He looks at a portrait over the mantelpiece as if into a mirror and straightens his tie.

An old beggar falls slowly out of the closet. The girls kick their legs and the clouds move. Statue of Liberty moves slightly.

end of period one

Position 2

The same but the gentleman takes a position on the wet dance floor.

The three girls on the shelf slide down the slide. They kick the beggar.

Two stand at the mantel while a third starts to dance with the gentleman.

The saxophonist plays.

The elephant enters, clumsily asks the girls for a dance, which they do not understand. The elephant passes them to contemplate the fallen beggar.

The clouds move. The Statue of Liberty moves across the floor on its rollers to stand of the elephant and beggar.

The elephant has taken the beggar up beside him on the sofa. They are comforting each other and exchanging confidences.

The two girls who are not dancing get into an argument. They draw knives and stab each other to death, fall dead and remain so.

Dim lights and a thousand mirrors like at the Hollywood Dance Palace.

The couple dance in the water, making ripples and reflections.

end of period two

Position 3

Dancers freeze at far end. Elephant and beggar fall over on floor. Liberty droops. The two women continue lying still.

Period 3: *Atlantis*

The Ocean Liner begins to rise, first from the bow and then evenly up.

Sound of cashregisters. The lights are dim. Murmurings from the beggar and the elephant.

The clouds pass and repass. They are squirted w. blue liquid and drip or are made to "rain".

The dancers sag into the water.

Fan blows air into the room.

The ship droops at the stern and sinks down to the floor. The walls are sprayed with red which runs down.

A flickering semidarkness as when watching TV at nite with the lites out . . .

end of period three
and end of Store Days II, Room 3

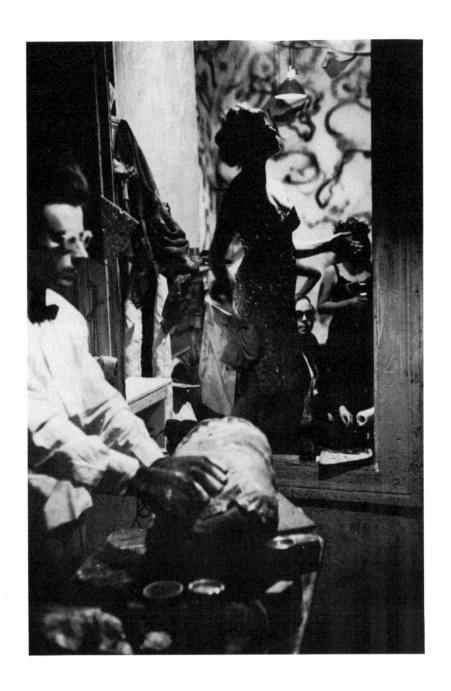

Second Draft

Store Days II

Marty
Steve

1. Cake
Marty alone. Sits on bed eating cake, which she leaves a piece of on the bed. Hears mouse near wall. Gets up and sets trap. Catches a fly or two. Returns to bed, sitting on cake. Smears. She wipes it up gently with a piece of paper, off her pants and the bed. Reads a magazine then throws it down, walks across room to turn on radio. Checks mousetrap. Steve enters, drops some beer cans out of a wet bag which clank on floor and goes out again.

2. Comics
She makes herself up in the mirror furtively, bizarrely, comic book in hand. Takes poses derived therefrom, wrestles lions etc. Is thrown against wall. Lips tremble. She coughs, breaks her acting, walks around and then sits down on bed and scrunches up against wall. Steve enters and makes a phone call and leaves a lot of objects on the floor old flowers etc.

3. War
She takes out a paint set and paints her pillows. She sits down with them. She takes off her shoes and polishes them. Steve enters and sits down. He tells her about his war experiences. She remains detached, from time to time directing what she believes a very penetrating look at him from under, which he doesnt receive, shines her shoes, runs her jewelry around her arms and neck and rearranges the nuts and bolts in the bed.

4. Mouse Trap
Steve sings. Reads comic book. She writes love letters quickly and clumsily, looks slyly at him (but not seeing him, a mannerism). Puts some letters under mattress, throws some at him. This doesnt reach him. He unties his shoes and stuffs them with paper. He puts them in the corner and walks around with holes in his socks. He steps on tacks, hurts his foot. He makes an urgent phone call. Marty checks her mousetrap, catches flies, arranges her pillows and the objects on the bed.

5. Tears
She cleans up the bed sweeps off the cake pieces, torn letters nuts & bolts etc. and takes a broom and sweeps around the bed. She sits down on the bed and reads. Steve unpacks his bag, all sorts of stuff. She cries a little, to the wall. Steve takes out newspaper. Marty checks mousetrap. She kneels on the bed looking out window. Steve comes up behind her in a not at all sinister way, matter of factly with a knife.

6. Kisses

He slides down the elastic on her puffed sleeves so that the back is bare, touches her here and there on the back with the blade, like kisses. Then with coins and mirrors, all of which he leaves on the bed. He goes out. Marty sits down, brushes off all these things now on the bed. She takes off blouse. She checks the mousetrap, table, her pillows etc. etc.

ROOM 2   STATION 2

Lucas
Cora

1. Sausages

Lucas climbs down from the attic wearing evening jacket. Cora is on floor. He examines meat hanging from ceiling in room. He spits on the floor. He goes to wash hands. The sink fills with red. He shines up and puts on his silver glasses. Pushes Cora aside and goes to table and starts stuffing small sausages.

2. The Phone

The phone rings. The butcher stops stuffing. He moves Cora to other side of room and goes to answer it. Blood runs down: Yes Yes Yes Yes Yes Yes Yes Yes Yes Yes etc. etc. fast. He slams receiver down. Goes back to table and starts removing pins which hold together roast pieces. Nails which hold together wood pieces. Cora hums. He says: shut up!

3. Books

He hangs up pieces of roast. Takes off and on glasses, polishes them. Takes out huge scissors and cuts phone book into square parts, ties them together. Hums. Sprinkles them with white paint and blue and then piles them carefully. He mounts ladder and lays the packs upstairs. He brings down a pile of fresh phone books.

4. The Cleaver

He takes down a huge cleaver, a piece of mirror and brandishes it in the flashing light. Cora burps. Shut up! he says. The phone rings. He moves her again. Answers it. Blood runs down. Yes Yes Yes Yes Yes Yes Yes Yes etc. Returns to table.Cleaves books. Cleaver flashes tears books apart. He piles them neatly. Hums. Crushes bulbs. Carefully with cleaver sweeps them into box. Salts them. Cuts metal artistically with shears.

5. A Bucket

Picks up Cora and maneuvers her onto table. She slips off. The phone rings again. Yes Yes Yes Yes Yes Yes etc. etc. Leaves phone hang, puts up Cora again. Swears, she falls off again. Hangs up phone in a pool of blood. Pushes her up but she falls, up but falls. Trips over a bucket of blood which splashes, Cora falls off, leaves it all and starts to shave.

6. Shaving

Leaves off shaving. Reaches up to attic with shave cream still on and begins to hand down gigantic eighteen foot man leg then another leg arm trunk. All kinds of stuff comes down also. Thighs now and chest arms head, it fills the whole room displacing the hanging meat. He begins forcing it into rooms I and III . . .

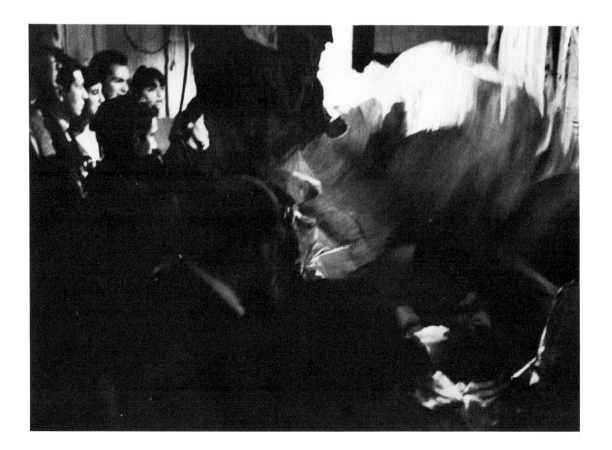

ROOM 3   STATION 3

Mickey
Jackie

1. Toys

Mickey sits on edge of dance floor facing audience, sipping out of a pepsi bottle. Jackie is above on shelf with a bunch of toys sewn of muslin, a ship, a sailboat, the city of NY upside down etc. a flag. A hand. She dangles them between her dangling legs and rolls down her stockings. and rolls them up again. Mickey takes hose and sprays floor which rearranges all the objects there: old shoes, papers, butts, mud etc. etc. She picks up certain objects in a burlap bag. sets it aside and sits down, fanning herself.

2. The Paper

Jackie throws down objects one by one on dance floor. Mickey takes out paper reads it. Jackie taps at it with her toes and teases Mickey from above. Mickey throws down paper and dances. Jackie applauds. Jackie reads paper, Mickey dances on. She piles the objects up bending over and kicks a few small pieces off the floor.

3. The Broom

Jackie lying seductively. Mickey starts to sweep the floor with bloody broom trailing all sorts of debris. Hard work. She sips from pepsi bottle. Jackie changes position, she drops her shoes and tries to get down. But she is afraid. Mickey ignores her sits down and reads the paper. Jackie sticks feet into paper, ignored by Mickey. She hesitates pretends wants help but finally draws herself back up.

4. A Customer

Henry arrives. He pays in pebbles covered with dirt which Mickey drops in her dress. Two turns, that's all. He leaves. Jackie stretches down to her. She climbs down on her back. Mickey sits down. Jackie walks around freely. Henry reappears, mud again, for Jackie quick waltz very tender. Henry leaves.

5. Knives

The girls dance, yawning Jackie sings She pulls a knife, they fight a little bit. Mickey sits down and reads the paper. Mickey ignores her.

6.

Jackie changes to mans costume, then to elephant costume. Throws her toys up on shelf and climbs after. Throws stuff down on dance floor again spitefully. Mickey is playing the tambourine.

3

Henry
Gloria
Rachel

1. Philosophy
Henry sits at table facing audience cutting strange shaped animals from big sheets of paper, following a line, saying hum hum. Gloria with two hand mirrors to his left is looking at her frame in the bl. dress. Rachel at mantel back playing with the objects there.

2. Cut-outs
Henry pins up the cutouts over the mantelpiece, Sticks self. Ouch. Gloria lies down rigidly on her back and pts her legs red white and blue. Rachel chokes Henry and stabs Gloria. She takes off her dress, but Henry and Gloria simply go on with their business, Henry cutting more stuff and Gloria painting her arms.

3. Wealth
Henry takes out a bag of silver cans and begins counting them. Gloria paints her face red white and blue like an indian. She paints a book silver, page by page and the covers sets it up to dry, coughs and sneezes. She brushes her teeth. Rachel stabs Henry several times.

4. A Lecture
Henry pulls out a rubber lecture which he cuts out and ties together and then hangs up over the mantelpiece. Gloria moves on her back inching over the floor to silver pedestal. She exercises her legs. Rachel sticks a long tube in her mouth. Henry looks at clock and goes to dance floor. Rachel knocks down all the objects on the mantelpiece.

5. A Song
Rachel gets up on pedestal to sing, but no song. Uses cards of smiles. Gloria gets up brushes herself sits on lower step of her pedestal, then sits herself up on next, turns on light and graciously takes her places, with attributes etc. Henry returns with enormous cards with girlies on them. He plays solitaire. Suddenly he stiffens, his eyes roll and his head hangs back (dead). Gloria smiles, wipes her nose with the torch and scratches herself with the book.

6.
She hangs up her attributes (Gloria) and descends, she falls too (dead). Rachel kicks the cans around the floor. She lights a cigarette. She puts on a big man's shirt. Kicks cans again. Sits down. Grabs Henry's ear, looks away. Runs thru her box of smiles.

Room 3   Independent station (6)

1. Tomatoes

Film begins. Pat enters, looks for seat, feels chair, above and Below. Sits down. Claes comes after, sits down, slumps in chair. Both watch film. Claes falls asleep, head rolls. Pat leaves. Returns as vaudeville entertainer quickly (she turns on lite from toilet) goes back. Cascade of tomatoes etc. Returns to audience

2. Pickpocket

Pat looks under chair, feels in Claes' pockets, pulls out stuff. Pretends to sleep, when Claes awakens. Looks in back pockets etc. Man wakes up, takes off his hat. Pat pretends to sleep. The two continue watching the empty screen.

3. New Seat

Pat sleeping. Claes feels his pants, gets up and goes out. Pat tries his seat—no good, wriggles ass in it. Gets back in old seat. Stuffs objects in pocket she had taken and from floor too. Claes returns. Pat excuses herself, enters again quickly as a dancer. Claes sleeps. lights cascade of tomatoes etc. Pat returns, sits down, sleeps.

4. Affection

Claes wakes up, starts to talk to Pat. His breath smells. She leans away from him. She excuses herself, goes out, lights on. She returns as vaudeville. Out and lights off. She comes back in, slumps in seat. He puts his arm around Pat. She knocks it off. He casts his head back and forth. Pat excuses herself.

5. Coins

Pat comes in in vaudeville. This time she touches and plays to Claes. She does things to curtain, other objects a la stripper etc. He snaps his fingers. She out lights off. She comes back shuffling, trips on him. He hits her. She scares him by putting two coins in her eyes and cackling. He laughs, he hides face, goes to sleep.

6. Magic

Claes gets up feels his pants, leaves. Pat the same. The film goes on. They come back in lights etc., as magician and assistant. He makes her disappear. Tomatoes, etc. They return one by one and fall asleep together.

7 The signed C is a leg on side.

Equals

Hair——Chicago
Hair——Bacon   Bacon——Flag
Hair——Phone
(Butt)erfly——Ham*bur*ger (BUttocks)
Sail——Mountain——Pie   Pie——Cap——Ship (from side)
                                    Pie——A——Crotch——Cone (w. circle)
                                    (fr. top)
Hat——Mouth (Lips)——Banana Split——Cup——Gun (Cap)
        Mouth——Hamburger (Mouth to Buttocks)   Cap——Ham
Frankfurter in Bun——Airplane (Saus*age* turned to Fusel*age*——
        Newspaper
Earrings——Airplane Wheels——Brassiere——Breasts
Fuselage——Ice Cream Cone——Wonder Bread (perspective)——Thigh
Layer Cake——Flag——(Pie)
Iwo Jima Monument——Pie——Battleship
Propeller——Frankfurter or Hamburger (rel. to Cowling)
Plane——Flower——Mirror
Hamburger——Watch in Case——Teeth (False)
Toaster (popup)——Cigarettes out of pack (pop up)
Trylon & perisphere——Coliseum Bldg——Ray Gun
Train——Belt (Tunnels)
Hamburger Meat——Head (Bun Hat) "Hamburger with head off"
Double popsicle——garter belt——
                        garter belt——bridge
Girdle——Cathedral
Watch——Apple
Shoe——Baked Potato——Coffin   Butter——Body
Obelisk——Ironing Board

boredom is beautiful
but it is hard to keep awake

cosmic somnolence
caused by the passing of a ship
thru water
birds thru skies
the sun across
the firmament

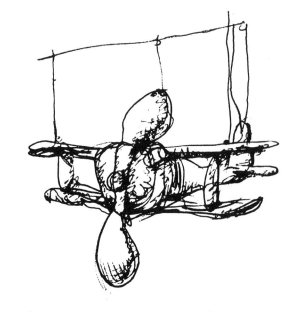

Portrait

The object in this case is a human being. His outward and inward
present and past components. He will be pickpocketed of these & a composition attempted.
A box of the analyzed components or their relatives, subject to altered circumstances, moving around, movable.

Kinetic in art means for me more than physical movement. It means
movement in time and identity and relation, an imaginary activity. Un-
limited this way. I prefer the physical movement in the spectator too not in
the work. Its definition depends on his position in time and space and in
imagination.

He invents the work.

Whitman is concerned primarily with time. There is about him a time
sense which is frightening. He is the master of nothing happening. He is
supersensitive to silences and long periods. He is wrapped in time.

Stage = place where I paint.

To fuse memory and present, that is my goal. Store equals both present and memory. Incarnate memory, the dream of art.

The year is also divided into 2 parts. Action and memory. An art primarily of action (present). An art of memory (past). Now one dominates now the other.

The Store can be both.

The Store is My Art.

Ray-Gun———my poetic power, my vision.

In different guises: The Store, The Street.

Each has phases, as I have phases. Moods, often contradictory.

Respect seasons respect nature respect self. Identification w. season with nature.

Memory begins to assume dominance about Aug. 1. Detachment increases, culminating in isolation later in year. Thus Blackouts, dealing as I introduced them with Time.

Easier to like this period.

Summer begins in action and ends in memory. More abrupt change than other seasons———winter/spring, fall/winter. The statement of summer is finally memorial, tho it doesnt appear to be. It culminates in August. Hence general sentimental loss sense assoc. with summer. If summer were planned for June–July, & Aug considered autumnal, it would be difft.

The action phase of the Store is stated in the Jaxon statement. The memory stage still to be written. In Store I try to sustain form or place or environment thru several phases as w. the Street.

funny the girdle became the symbol of a direction in many ways
none more surprising than as an example of form———material———the thin and white (plaster) crust or stiffened cloth (as with stays) at the same time as it became the pointer in the direction of erotic imagery involving both merchandise and the female body

I find that on beginning a piece or a performance I have a lot on my mind none of which is finally true until it has collided with the facts of making. As I proceed all the thought that does not work is discarded and what is retained is so mixed up with the facts of realization that it ceases to be expressible verbally. At the completion of my work I'm afraid I have nothing to say at all. That is I have either thrown it away or used it up.

What is a hat 6 ft high?

The only defense against being trapped in someones idea of your intention is to keep changing your field and work very hard, so that the *fact* of your creation, which will always be the most important thing, always overshadows its interpretation.

Not forget I am a sculptor

My personal struggle has been to return painting to the tangible object, which is like returning the personality to touching and feeling the world around it, to offset the tendency to vagueness and abstraction. To remind people of practical activity, to suggest the senses and not escape from the senses, to substitute flesh and blood for paint. If I have gone too far in the classical fallacy of confusing reality and art, I beg pardon on account of my enthusiasm.

The studio for making art goes thru different guises, now a store,
next year perhaps a factory

How are real pants made?

I do not think the object-maker need worry himself about where he shows. F.ex. that he should worry about showing his objects in an "art" gallery or a museum, or that his objects will inevitably be misrepresented and priced and exploited as "art". He hasnt much choice and if his idea is strong enough it will overwhelm the place where it is presented. Nothing is more appropriate than that a revolutionary idea be presented in the place which is under attack, provided of course that it can be done freely. Some disguises may be necessary. Certain initial compromises provided they do not compromise the eventual aim.

Crucial point is of course that at center of my use of pop art is a love for the rejected, inexplicable and simple. The City Venus and this strange devotion——from this everything else follows.

Aagh my pompous explanations of art, and isolating the essence of art, as offensive to me as to other artists.

back to my realism to my view of the world my shit view

My motives are so veiled to me that I dont think I can provide much in the way of being helpful and truthful about what I have done. My work mystifies me, and I would not want to know what I am doing, even if I could. Also what people see may be more important than what I see, and what they see is after all the test, even if they dont see it right away. I wouldn't want to prejudice anyone, or try to make them see what isnt there.

I speak through the drawings, the sculptures and all the things I make and through my theater, and I dont like to hear myself in words.

you know that disguises are very important to me,
for the purpose of example.
I wish all my actions to be exemplary

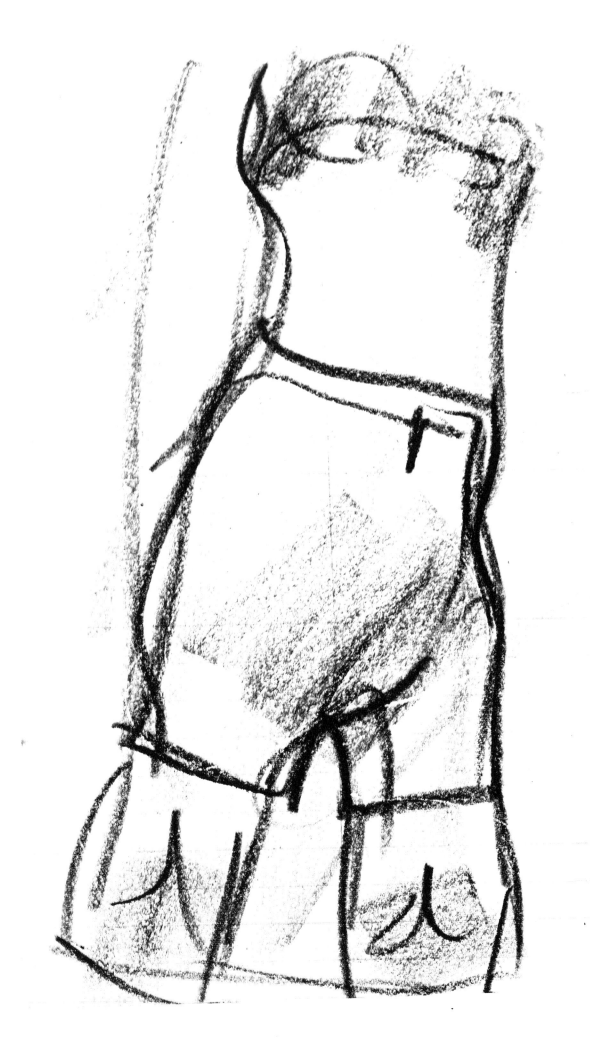

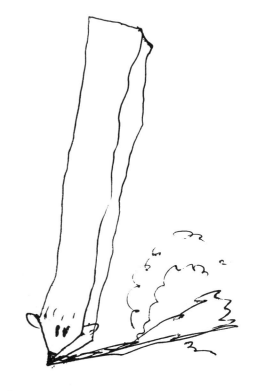

MON = MOUSE =
PENCIL =
PIE = ?

IWO MON =
BATLSHP =
PIE

          Teddy bears jump
          tump i dump dump
          jump i dump tumpi
          dum dump
          jeddy bears tump jump
          teddy bears jump

Things have a rancid flavor.
Everyone seems to be going away. We should have gone away.
psychology (my specialty)
The house is in need of repair, and furniture. Now that all the stuff is out,
theres no furniture! We didn't realize that. We havent the money to buy new
either.
The place will never look like a home no matter what we do. Meantime
there are leaks and the refrigerator doesnt work and the usual bugs and
whoo!

Its lack of money that makes you sad, thats for sure.
At the store, theres so much to do, and without the conviction that its
worth it. Take from precious cash.

O in summer all things go to hell. One gets stretched.

love scene
Armistice
the blast in the gasworks
the sinking mill
the ruin

Mythic voyages. Interiors.

Keep the store open a half year and then sell it whole.

Get me a commission to be transferred into bronze.

The audience comes in directly, finds places. Meanwhile Lucas is sweeping the floor which is covered with sand, throwing down new sand, and mixing with this blue dry pigment. The lighting is blue, neurasthenic. Slivers of mirrors hang by string along the wall. Above are forms of stuffed muslin, like sausages or clouds, tied up like garlands. Lucas is dressed as a waiter, in a white costume.

When the table is set, with a plastic flower in a silver bottle in the middle and a blue and white tablecloth, Lucas announces the beginning of the piece rather formally. The names of the parts, the names of the actors and the violinist.

John may enter before or after the announcement. He sits down facing the large mirror. White face and a baggy suit. He rises to play his interlude.

The three relatives enter, sit down around the table. Lucas serves them. They talk, to themselves, to each other, to Lucas, in different languages. Öyvind-Swedish, Maricla-Portuguese and Irene-Spanish. Lucas responds from time to time in Greek.

Pat enters into the middle room and makes the bed, which up to now has been covered with a black cloth. The bed is full of talcum. As she shakes the mattress and covers, the dust rises, fills the room. The relatives go on eating and talking. She makes the bed nicely. She wears little girl pajamas with elephants on them. Having made the bed nicely, she leaves.

An ugly monster, Claes in a burlap costume enters, swinging its limbs around nervously into the audience, paws at the bed and finally climbs into it.

Action ceases in all rooms. End of first part.

John who has been in his chair throughout, rises, plays his interlude, slowly, deliberately as before. Sits down.

Part Two: The Bride

The relatives resume their eating and talking and business. Maricla takes off her blue stockings and bathes her feet in a pan on the floor. Öyvind kills a fly or two. Irene tries on flat cardboard masks. Etc.

Milet, dressed as the groom, enters. He fixes his tie and hair in the mirror in front of the violinist, has a few words with him, and then goes into the middle room. He finds the monster sleeping in the bed. Milet pokes the monster. He throws back the covers and pushes the monster out of bed, chases him around the bed. He kicks the monster and chases it out of the room.

He sets the bed straight. He leaves to get his Bride.

He pulls the Bride (Pat) in slowly. She is wrapped in wrapping paper painted white, with a mask under a cowl like a nun, and tied with twine. He pulls her down the corridor into the bedroom. He undoes or cuts the twine with a pocketknife.

Under the paper statue, Pat is dressed in a crepe shift. He takes the bouquet out of her hand, lays her on the bed and removes the crepe costume, tearing it down the center and laying it aside.

A sort of elation comes over him. He walks rather vaguely into the room of the relatives, stopping to exchange a few words with the violinist and straightens his tie. He takes a bottle of wine and sits down at the table with the relatives. They pay no attention to him. He toasts them and talks to them, in Yugoslavian. They go on about their business.

He gets up and returns to the bedroom, stopping again to talk to the violinist and straightens his tie. He lifts Pat from the bed and carries her out.

He returns and rather drunkenly stuffs the bed with beer cans painted silver and feathers from a bag hanging over the bed.

He staggers into the relatives' room, again pausing by the violinist to talk, straighten his tie. Sits down, drinks, talks, etc. But the action soon subsides. End of second part.

John rises to play his interlude.

Part Three: The Relatives

A record begins to play (Lucas turns it on), of Hawaiian selections, The Hawaiian Wedding Song, Blue Hawaii, Aloha Oe, a 33 rpm record at 16 rpm, taking about 18 minutes to play through the three pieces.

This is a very long time under the circumstances. After about ten minutes, the far part of the audience is "released"—the ropes holding them back are removed, and they crowd up to the last room where the slow action goes on.

All the action is in the most intense slow motion. It should take the full time for Lucas to pass the seven or so feet from offstage to the table and set down the tray he is carrying on the table. The objects are fastened to the tray by strings, so that they can only fall a short distance. To keep the objects involved under control, in time, will be the biggest problem.

Lucas already has a mask on, made of aluminum paper sprayed white.

The Relatives put on masks made on the spot at the beginning of the part. They crush the aluminum paper into their faces, making rough masks.

Maricla who should be standing, having given her chair to Milet, has a bamboo stick with a crayon in it, with which she draws an outline around her body and arm and hand and fingers. This should take her 18 minutes.

Irene applies makeup, especially lipstick, to her mask. This should take her 18 minutes. Öyvind unfolds a large map of the universe, full of symbols, which eventually covers the whole table. This should take him 18 minutes.

Lucas enters, walks, sets the tray down, bends over it. That takes him 18 minutes.

When the record has played out, the Relatives and Milet remain frozen in their positions. From this time to the end they are as dead, needing only a touch or a shove to fall or break apart.

Lucas leaves the room. John rises to play his interlude.

Part Four: The Bears

Lucas returns, a towel on his arms. He walks on crates, bending over to set one after another in front of him, which raises him high above the table. He drags a large muslin bag and when he reaches the table, he begins to clear it of the many objects which have gathered there.

A commotion in the other end, behind the audience. Pat and Claes in burlap costumes, enter struggling. Boxing, wrestling and rubbing the bottoms of their shoes in the sand on the floor. Shoving the audience, throwing nervous punches in all directions. Gradually, they make their way through the audience and into the last room.

The mirror slivers are set swinging, the large mirror is turned awry. As their fighting approaches and threatens the table, Lucas swats them with his towels. However, the Bears ignore the blows, wrapped up in their fighting.

Inevitably, their fighting intrudes on the table. The relatives are knocked over and the table top is tipped off. The chairs fall. Lucas swats at the Bears furiously, finally drives them off, and they run out.

Lucas leaves. The room is a mess. The violinist rises and plays his interlude. End of the fourth part and *Nekropolis II.*

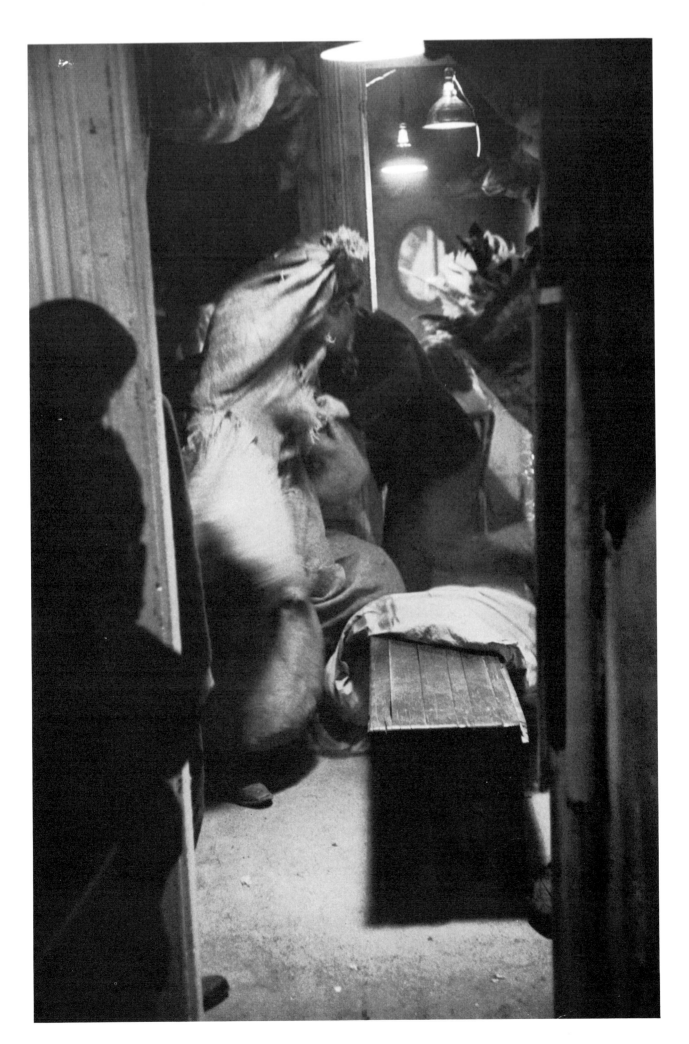

Report on The Store

The store was open to the public from Dec. 1 through Jan. 31, two months, rather than the one month which was planned.

Sales in this period totaled $1655 (as itemized). Of this amount, $300 is still owed. I will bill for this.

No sales tax was computed in the sales.

The expenses for the store, excluding electric bill, not yet received, total $368, ~~somewhat under the anticipated $400.~~ This (as itemized) includes construction, telephone, photos, utilities, publicity and printing, but not the cost of addressing and mailing, ~~Perhaps with the addition~~ addition of which ought to bring the amount near the anticipated $400.

The gallery agreed to pay half the expenses and take a commission of one third on all sales above $200, or my share of expenses.

Thus: Sales   1655.00
                   - 200.00
                    1455.00   1/3 of $1455.00 - $485.00

                                            - 200.00
                                              285.00

I owe the gallery $285.00.

~~Sales~~ tax on sales, to be paid: 49.65   285.00
                                                  49.65
                                                 334.65

MON'S SOUV'S

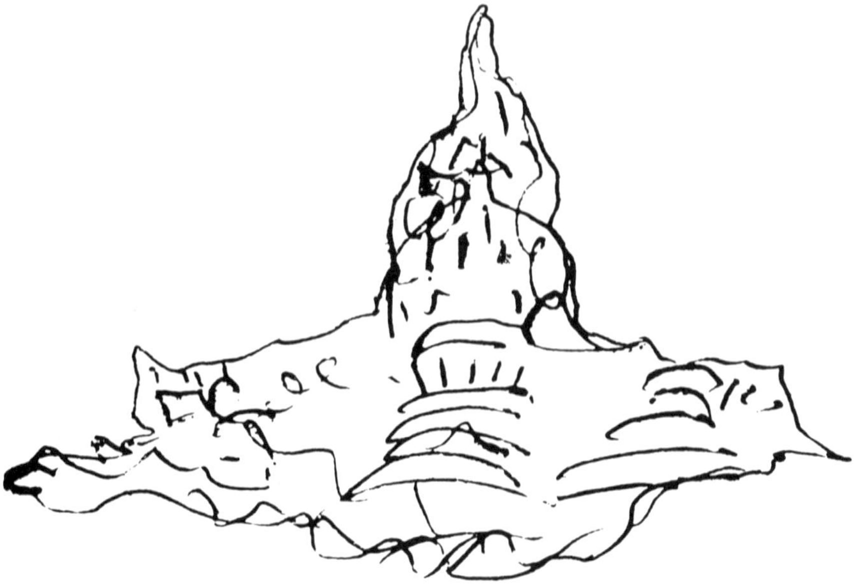

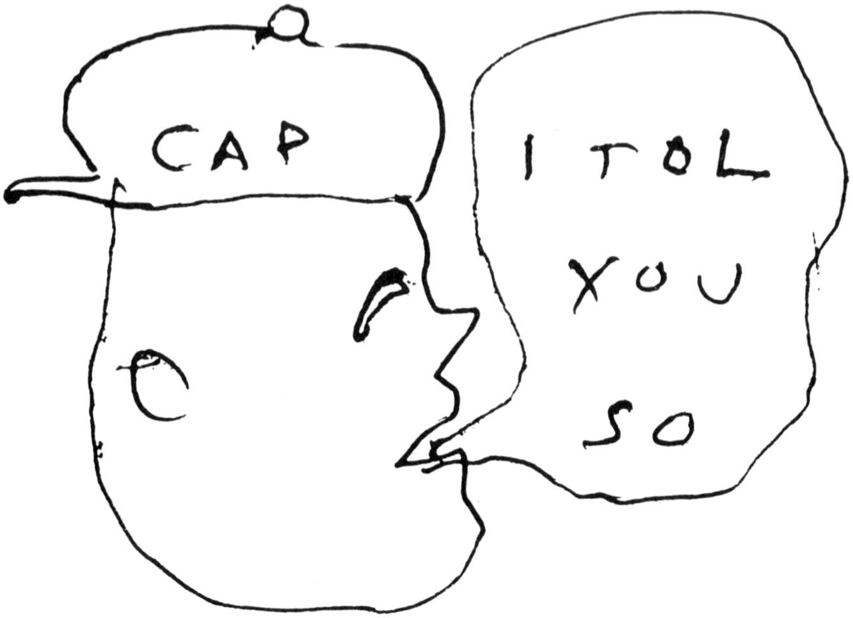